DISCUSSIONS *of* SPIRITUAL ATTUNEMENT *&* SOUL EVOLUTION

Volume II

AKHENATON

THE PORTAL PRESS
Columbia, Maryland

To the unfoldment of
The Wisdom of One -

Akhenaton

CONTENTS

11

12

PREFACE

This text is the second volume in a series of question and answer texts designed to help illuminate several aspects of Spiritual Conscience that can assist mankind in the process of assimilating The Wisdom of One. Taken from questions and areas of concern that frequently arise during our Sunday Spiritual Gatherings and from Spiritual Counseling/Facilitation Sessions at Portal Enterprises, the subject areas that we engage in this text range from basic principles and definitions of Enlightenment, the Soul, Intuitive Wisdom, Fear, Grace and God-realization to more profound, complex and/or esoteric subjects that include discussions of the Ego-self, Healing Facilitation, Karmic Resolution, the Akasha, Maya, the God-self, the nature and function of the Chakra System and The Council of Twelve.

In this text, we discuss principles and make statements that at first glance may appear to be difficult to comprehend or to accept, but the earnest seeker of enlightenment will not be deterred by that which appears to be an obstacle to comprehension and learning. The earnest seeker of enlightenment will allow his/her intuition and conviction to penetrate the veil of illusion that clouds understanding to find the shimmering essence of Truth awaiting discovery.

For many soul incarnates, the societal conditioning imposed upon mortal consciousness has obscured and

13

in some cases has aggressively discouraged the practice of many principles that were once an integral part of early man's practice of Spiritual Conscience. An example of this tendency is the historical use of governmental sanctions, be they military, Religious or bureaucratic, to shape the belief systems and to define the behavior patterns of the masses. This pattern of conditioning can also be seen in the manner in which man has nearly extinguished the sense of reverence and respect for the abundance and the beauty of Mother Earth that was once a basic principle of mortal life. Exploiting Mother Earth in the name of capitalism and industrialism, man has instead come to look upon The Earth Mother as a source of riches and personal wealth and in so doing, has severely damaged the very foundation of mortal life.

Pressures and emotional inclinations to conform to "accepted standards of behavior" have had immeasurable impact upon the drives of the ego-self and man's subsequent willingness to embrace belief systems that were validated by the ruling classes. In effect what this means is that in an attempt to survive and to prosper upon Mother Earth, man has accepted the self-serving, judgemental, repressive attitudes imposed by those in positions of authority. This acceptance has conditioned mortal man to see and to primarily believe in those aspects of mortal existence that can be verified by rational processes. Therefore, if one cannot touch, taste, smell, hear, see or validate reality with the linear

14

thought process, then one tends to doubt, deny or dismiss the occurrence of events outside the established parameters of experience. This tendency toward shortsightedness has caused much of mankind to label the pursuit of Spiritual Conscience as the practice of primitive superstition and witchcraft or practices that sustain fantasy and delusion. In either case, modern man's ability to comprehend or to explain the occurrence of phenomena not promulgated by Occidental Traditions is severely inhibited.

This text is designed to provide mankind with a viable tool to assist in the re-accessing, re-awakening or re-attuning to the inherent, intuitive Spiritual Knowledge that lies dormant in the collective consciousness of mortal man. By offering Timeless Truths to those soul incarnates who wish to contemplate Spiritual Unfoldment, we have attempted to render services born of Universal Conscience unto the hearts and souls of our brethren inhabiting The Earth Mother. By placing elements of The Wisdom of One at the disposal of mankind for conscionable discernment, we have attempted to return unto The Body of Creation the Love and understanding that we have enjoyed in physical life. We have accepted the task of assisting those soul incarnate beings who do not enjoy the same clarity of perception and abiding Love that fills us in accessing The Light of One, that which is the source of illumination and the impetus by which every step of Soul Evolution eventuates. It is our purpose and continuing effort, in some small way, to facilitate the evolution of those who seek Spiritual Truth. Through the energy, inspiration and information offered in texts such as this and by The Grace of The Universal One, each conscious vibration of life, each soul incarnate being, will in time come to appreciate his/her inextricable, God-illumined connection to all things born of Creation - for in Truth, all things exist as One.

Shalom, Adonai, Shalom

Akhenaton

DISCUSSIONS *of* SPIRITUAL ATTUNEMENT & SOUL EVOLUTION

Volume II

*"Enlightenment is
an ongoing process by
which The Wisdom or
The Conscience of One
is awakened
and brought into
crystalline focus
in the consciousness
of mortal man."*

One

Q: *Akhenaton, how do you define "Enlightenment"?*

A: Most speak of enlightenment as a state of being, a blissful, lofty existence that is somewhat detached from Earthly Reality, but such an assessment of enlightenment is largely inaccurate, as it lacks a practical avenue for the application of evolved consciousness to daily life upon The Earth Mother. Enlightenment is neither a state of detached consciousness that one experiences as a result of Earthly tasks completed, nor is enlightenment a condition of bliss that one attains as a result of learning The Lessons of Existence; rather, enlightenment is an ongoing process by which The Wisdom or The Conscience of One is awakened and brought into crystalline focus in the consciousness of mortal man. Further, it is not that many lessons are to be processed in the journey toward enlightenment, but that only a few basic precepts of Universal Law are to be acknowledged and conscionably applied to all aspects of mortal existence.

One who seeks enlightenment is a student of the Universe, its function and all things born of Creation and also endeavors to find and maintain Peace and Harmony through the reincarnate journey of Soul

Evolution. It is the student of enlightenment who inevitably becomes his/her own teacher, as attunement to one's own Intuitive Voice grows sharper and more dynamic. It is the "God-self" to which one attunes, thereby accessing one's eternal and personal connection to The Infinite Body of God. To comprehend the nature of the path toward enlightenment requires that one understand the applications of the precepts of Universal Law: Patience, Compassion, Wisdom, Mercy, Serenity and Altruistic Love in The Light of One. To implement These Precepts is to practice heart-centered, enlightened behavior and to live within The Conscience of One. During the process of implementing These Divine Precepts, mankind facilitates the unfoldment of enlightenment and subsequently fills each moment of life with joy, wonderment and Divine Conscience.

Enlightenment is a purposeful, Divine Process through which the limited vision of mortal consciousness is slowly transformed and broadened, expanded in such a way as to allow mankind to discover The True Spirit of God alive in all things born of Creation. As one becomes progressively more illuminated by The Truth of The God Spirit, no longer do third dimension drives of ego direct the course of life. Thought and behavior patterns become more altruistic, patient and understanding, as one becomes a willing, less reactionary participant in the unfoldment and assimilation of The Wisdom of One.

As man finds reason to allow him/herself to flow with the current of life, the path of Truth clearly unfolds, allowing the earnest seeker to simply choose those avenues that he/she knows through heart-centered analysis to be "good and right". It is the seeker of enlightenment who ultimately finds that the omnipresence of The God Spirit is at once simple to define, yet beyond the scope of explanation. And too does the seeker find that within the omnipresence of The God Spirit lies the potential of mortal man's Divine Consciousness patiently awaiting the moment of discovery.

*"It is the expression of
The Conscience of One
that ultimately leads
mankind toward the
acknowledgement
and acceptance
of God-realization."*

Two

Q: *What is "The Conscience of One"?*

A: The Conscience of One, also known as The Wisdom of One and The Law of One, is the application of the principle that all things born of Creation contain the same Life/Light Vibration or Divine Consciousness and that all things upon Planet Earth, as well as all things throughout the galactic realm of existence, should be afforded the Blessings of Love, Patience, Compassion, Wisdom, Mercy and Serenity. It is for each evolving soul incarnate being to understand and to accept the proposition that there is a place and a function for all things born of Creation within The God's Divine Order. Additionally, mankind, as the most evolved of The God's third density beings, has a custodial responsibility to engage and to manage the other Kingdoms upon Mother Earth with a sense of Compassion and Understanding firmly anchored in the application of Universal Law.

It is The Conscience of One that guides mankind with Absolute Truth toward more and more heart-centered, Light-minded behavior. It is the comprehension and the application of The Conscience of One that gently extinguishes counterproductive, egocentric behaviors, as mortal consciousness is surrendered to The Greater Will of The One. And it is the expression of The Conscience of One that ultimately leads mankind toward the acknowledgement and acceptance of God-realization. You see, it is through man's own conscious choice to forgive and to release discordance and painful emotional memories that man can approach the time of readiness to embrace the vision of mankind's benevolent, purposeful, Godly nature, for as a direct result of the assimilation of The Conscience of One, each mortal being approaches his/her personal moment to behold the vision of The Infinite Body of God.

"It is the soul
that is the 'spirit
consciousness' that
structures and directs
the scenarios of life,
unveiling The Lessons
of Existence that each
mortal being must
engage in order
to assimilate
The Wisdom of One."

Three

Q: *How do you define "Soul"?*

A: We define soul as the energy matrix or The Light
Vibration of Consciousness in which the memory of
reincarnate life experience is recorded. It is the soul
that is the "spirit consciousness" that structures and
directs the scenarios of life, unveiling The Lessons of
Existence that each mortal being must engage in order
to assimilate The Wisdom of One. Through the soul,
each incarnate being seeks expression of his/her indi-
viduality and displays an evolving conscious understanding of his/her personal connection to The Infinite
Body of God. It is through the expression of the soul
that mortal man observes those behavioral traits or
Karmic Patterns that require understanding, forgiveness and release and as the result of Soul Evolution,
mortal man engenders the blessings of Love and
Compassion in the treatment of all things born of
Creation.

It is through the culmination of the designs of evolution implemented by the conscious soul that man
observes the evolution of the God-self, for it is the pre-
incarnate choices that each mortal being makes at the
soul-level that determine the nature of life-events that

he/she will engage at each stage of incarnate existence. As has been implied, it is through the soul that one chooses to engage Karmic Debt in order to facilitate the Unfoldment Process. The awareness of such soul-level choices, more often than not, is unavailable to the conscious mind. Therefore, through directives of the ego-self, the conscious mind becomes busily engaged in structuring obstacles to impede the resolution of Karmic Debt that would allow greater expression of the God-self. Nevertheless, it is the deeper understanding of reincarnate processes available at the soul-level that is the impetus by which Divine Conviction and perseverance are awakened and sustained in the face of adversity. It is then that one begins to "feel" a higher purpose in operation through the travail and tribulation one perceives in life-events. It is then that one begins to understand the eternal nature of the soul and identifies the temporal nature of the ego-self. It is then that one begins to acknowledge and accept the Intuitive Wisdom of the soul that forms the evolved energy matrix of the heart-centered God-self.

" As the compelling drives of ego become extinguished, the soul incarnate begins to view life and the act of service with eyes of clarity and Compassion."

Four

Q: *What is the meaning of the term "Harvest",*
Akhenaton?

A: Harvest occurs at the end of each Karmic Cycle,
approximately every 65,000 years, and is the time during which the soul vibrations of mortal man can pass
from third dimension reality into fourth dimension
consciousness. In preparation for Harvest, many soul
incarnates choose to engage all past Karmic Debts in
one final, dramatic incarnation. When such a soul-
level, pre-incarnate choice is made, the soul incarnate
engages an ever-unfolding life-sequence that allows
him/her to confront those aspects of self that require
understanding, forgiveness, blessing and transmutation. Through such a process, each mortal being pre-
pares him/herself for the next phase of Soul Evolution
- accepting and applying fourth density principles of
"Christ-Consciousness".

It is for each mortal being to comprehend the precepts
of Christ-Consciousness while in third dimension. This
comprehension process will occur at a time that is good
and right in each soul incarnate's journey toward the
assimilation of The Wisdom of One, facilitating the
actual ascension process into fourth dimension reality.

Further, when one has ascended to fourth density consciousness, one no longer has need to reincarnate upon Earth. The Lessons of Existence will have been learned and the requirements for Karmic Resolution will have been fulfilled.

Upon learning of the time of Harvest and the promise of fourth dimension consciousness, most soul incarnates usually exclaim, *"Thank God! I won't be coming back to Earth again!"* or words to that effect. But what is most interesting is that as a soul incarnate learns more and more about heart-centered, Light-minded behavior and as the compelling drives of ego become extinguished, the soul incarnate begins to view life and the act of service with eyes of clarity and Compassion. It is then that many soul incarnate beings who vehemently and joyfully proclaimed freedom from subsequent Earthly incarnations choose to return to Mother Earth to assist the remaining children of Creation with the process of Soul Evolution. Such dramatic transformations in thought and behavior patterns demonstrate how the Enlightenment/Unfoldment Process gives birth to the true "God-illumined" nature of mortal man, which is the Divine expression of the God-self.

"The ego-self is
directed to seek
expression for
only those aspects of
mortal consciousness
that engage survival,
pleasure and personal
aggrandizement
states."

Five

Q: *Why is it that some people say that their Prayers go unanswered and that they rarely receive guidance through Meditation or vision?*

A: One can make repeated supplications to The God Spirit entreating The Omnipresent One for assistance, guidance or strength in overcoming discordant life-situations, but it will be to no avail if the supplicant is unable or has not yet reached the moment of readiness to assimilate those aspects of The Wisdom of One that will facilitate the personal surrender of mortal consciousness to The Greater Will of The One. It would be much the same as traveling to a mineral-rich, natural spring to collect nourishing water with a leaking bucket. No matter how many trips were made to the spring, upon returning home, one would always find the bucket empty, without the precious water that the journey had been undertaken to obtain. Even though seeing and tasting the mineral water were possible, securing a supply of the water was impossible, as the tool, the bucket, was faulty. Without the proper preparations, tools of understanding and faith in the Unfoldment Process, one can perpetually quest to attain or ask for that which one is unable to effectively utilize or incorporate into a viable expression of

37

his/her reality.

Additionally, it is not uncommon that the supplicant would ask The God Spirit to render Blessings and/or guidance that would be in keeping with that which the ego-self would accept and acknowledge as useful. The ego-self is directed to seek expression for only those aspects of mortal consciousness that engage survival, pleasure and personal aggrandizement states. But in anticipating a specific response from The God Spirit in a single-minded, linear fashion, it is most probable that the supplicant would not recognize a subtle, Divine Response when it is given. Indeed, mortal man can only receive that which he/she is ready and willing to accept.

Even when one thinks that he/she is entreating The God Spirit to intervene on the behalf of those thought to be in the midst of pain, suffering and degradation, it is the ego-self that will have compelled one to encroach upon the Free Will of others - even if the Free Will of others has been designed to choose painful scenarios by which to learn lessons that may not be immediately discernable to either those viewing the pain and suffering, or those experiencing it. Only when directly asked by the party or parties involved is it good and right to engage discordance on the behalf of another. (One notable exception to this point is the engagement of discordance on the behalf of another as a "selfless" act, sacrificing one's own physical/emotional well-being to save or to assist another soul incarnate being in a potentially life-threatening situation. In such cases, Karma can be engaged and resolved by all parties concerned.)

It is most important for all those who seek Spiritual Truth to find and nurture the seed of Patience alive within mortal consciousness, so that the application of Patience can become an integral part of mortal experience. By implementing Patience, each soul incarnate is better able to fathom the true purpose of the process of Spiritual Unfoldment, that which allows the surrender of the conscious will of man to The Greater Will Of The Universal One to occur as a natural process.

"Intuitive Wisdom is the guidance that each soul incarnate being receives through the functioning of an open, evolved heart chakra."

Six

Q: *Please define "Intuitive Wisdom" and explain the process by which this ability can be cultivated.*

A: Intuitive Wisdom or The Intuitive Voice is the accessible body of knowledge alive within the soul matrix of every incarnate being that is resultant from past incarnate experience and/or association. This is the reservoir of knowledge that can be used to effectively evaluate or can be conscionably applied to present and future incarnate situations. Intuitive Wisdom is the guidance each soul incarnate being receives through the functioning of an open, evolved heart chakra. It is through the process of Ego-transmutation and the conscious release of traumatic emotional memories associated with heart chakra function that the soul incarnate learns of the availability, value and application of Intuitive Wisdom.

To execute Intuitive Wisdom requires steadfast Conviction and faith in the reality of The One Infinite Creator alive in all things born of Creation. You see, it is through mankind's acceptance and understanding of Divine Presence that the expression of Godliness is facilitated through mortal thoughts and behaviors. It is

41

then that Intuitive Wisdom can be shown to be guidance and Truth born of Universal Conscience.

It is also important to note that conditioned behaviors of the ego-self constantly attempt to impugn the validity of Intuitive Wisdom. Whenever the conscious mind begins to probe and question that which is felt through the heart as Truth, then the purity of intuition can easily be compromised or sacrificed for the illusion of protection or for the maintenance of the illusion of importance of the ego-self. This is a process that every mortal incarnate has engaged or will engage at one time or another and will inevitably view as counterproductive in the evolution of self. To be sure, the time will come for each soul incarnate being to accept, embrace and follow the guidance of The Voice of God alive within his/her own conscious soul.

"We describe our approach to Spirituality as 'Trans-Cultural', born of many Traditions or roots, yet the many roots are the vehicles of nourishment for The One Tree of Knowledge..."

Seven

Q: Akhenaton, how do you describe your approach to Spirituality?

A: We describe our approach to Spirituality as "Trans-Cultural", born of many Traditions or roots, yet the many roots are the vehicles of nourishment for The One Tree of Knowledge, The One Tree of Life. From past incarnate experience, we have knowledge of many Spiritual, Mystical and Religious Traditions, all of which contain information and Wisdom of importance to the evolution of mankind's Spiritual Consciousness. We have not allowed any single Tradition to limit or to color our understanding or application of The Wisdom of One, thereby giving our sense of Spirituality an unfettered, unique freedom of expression.

Certainly the philosophy we promulgate is neither new, nor is it revolutionary. The philosophy we engage is contained and practiced in Hindu, Buddhist, Native American, West African, Christian, Judaic, Islamic, Asian and Mystical Traditions throughout the world. What we have done is to synthesize and refine the influences of many Traditions into a natural order of thought and behavior that can be implemented at any time, under any conditions and in any corner of the world.

We have not attempted to improve upon Traditions that have served the needs of mankind for thousands of years; rather, we have engaged those heart-centered motivations that have always been a part of Spiritual Conscience. We have engaged those precepts that are deemed to be good and right for the evolution and maintenance of all things. We have engaged the common bonds that connect all Traditions of Conscience to each other. We have engaged those aspects of many Traditions that proclaim all things born of Creation to be as One and have allowed Divine Truth to precipitate the subsequent expressions of our Spirituality.

Having chosen to embrace The Light of One and having chosen to embrace mortal consciousness with Patience, Compassion, Wisdom, Mercy, Serenity and Love, we most certainly also will have chosen to extract the most benevolent, the most functionally pure elements from any Tradition or philosophy to express through our application of Spiritual Conscience. To be sure, any mortal being who so chooses can access those heart-centered vibrations that bespeak Truth and Love and in so doing, display an understanding that allows the functional application of elements of ancient Spiritual Traditions to be made in conscionable acts of service.

"The Council of Twelve is the Etheric Unit responsible for the galactic plan of the Earth Colony."

Eight

Q: *Akhenaton, it is said that you are a conduit for an etheric group known as "The Council of Twelve". Who are The Council of Twelve and how did the process of conduit take place? What responsibilities does functioning as a conduit for The Council of Twelve carry?*

A: As a child, communion with Spiritual Energies occurred regularly, but at that time the actual source of the communication was not precisely known. Sometimes, voices would speak and direct the unsuspecting child to engage in counterproductive or destructive behaviors. Other times, Etheric Energy would wrap the child in glowing, comforting sensations that filled the heart with Love and Peace.

During adolescence and young adulthood, the learning process unfolded to allow intuitive identification to develop, which made it possible to distinguish between the trickery and admonitions of one group of Spiritual Energies and the pure, benevolent vibrations transmitted by the other group of Etheric Energies. Sometimes distinguishing between the two factions was extremely difficult, because the deception employed by one group at times could be very subtle, veiled by what appeared to be "goodness and truth".

49

After passing several "Etheric Initiations" that proved readiness to become an Initiate in The Light of One and readiness to accept the mantle of conduit, the conscious channeling that had always been allowed suddenly changed. Instead of hearing and repeating long monologues or dissertations from The Council, I, we, simply knew and understood specific principles that were and are the very heart-centered motivation of The Council of Twelve.*

The Council of Twelve is the Etheric Unit responsible for the galactic plan of the Earth Colony. During the days of Lemuria and Atlantis, The Council of Twelve was known as The Oversouls. The Council of Twelve is a group of twelve, individual, separately evolved, social memory complexes, each of whom vibrates at its own distinct resonance rate, but can and chooses to vibrate in harmony with the eleven others. Having evolved beyond the need for physical form, The Council exists as Light Energy Matrices of Divine Consciousness. The Yahweh Entity is one member of The Council of Twelve. Even though we were unaware of Its functional existence during the very early part of this incarnation, it has been The Yahweh Entity with Whom we have resonated and with Whom we have communicated all of this life.

For further information about The Council of Twelve, see "Chakra Sealing & The Council of Twelve" in Crystal Communion: LoveLight Meditations by Akhenaton.

50

The only responsibility that we have accepted in functioning as a conduit is to implement the precepts of Universal Law in ways that are conscionable and to assist mortal man in the Unfoldment Process that leads to the assimilation of The Wisdom of One. If effect, we have neither chosen, nor accepted any more or any less than any other Light-minded child of Creation will ultimately engage in the experience of third dimension reality.

"It would be in direct opposition to the precepts and directives of The Council of Twelve to override or in any way to compromise the Choice of Free Will of any soul incarnate being."

Nine

Q: *Does The Council of Twelve ever override your Intuitive Voice or redirect your sense of judgement?*

A: The Council of Twelve exists to guide the Earth Colony through the process of Spiritual Evolution in a manner that nurtures the natural unfoldment of Divine Consciousness within mortal man. It would be in direct opposition to the precepts and directives of The Council of Twelve to override or in any way to compromise the Choice of Free Will of any soul incarnate being. Further, the Intuitive Voice or Intuitive Wisdom is vital for the expression of man's soul consciousness and works in harmony with The Council to co-create the third dimension expression of Divine Truth. That is, the Intuitive Voice merges with the consciousness of The Council of Twelve to develop viable avenues to implement the precepts of Universal Law upon the Earth Plane.

It has never been the practice or policy of The Council of Twelve to engage mortal consciousness for the purpose of manipulating or controlling the behaviors of mortal man. The practices and designs of The Council have been and remain to engage the collective consciousness of mankind in ways that stimulate the awakening of Divine Truth that existed as part of the initial creative programming of modern man's birth consciousness. By allowing mankind to engage in behaviors that are discordant and/or counterproductive, The Council upholds the non-intervention policy that promotes Choice of Free Will and in so doing, The Council of Twelve also facilitates the moment of man's discovery and acceptance of behaviors that are more in keeping with the precepts of Universal Law. Further, upon man's discovery, acceptance and implementation of more benevolent, service-oriented behaviors, mankind's resonance rate or vibration of Spiritual Consciousness more closely approximates the rate of resonance of The Council of Twelve, which allows for direct and conscious communication to take place.

"... The Spiritual Path is chosen to help mortal man learn how to become One with all Universal Realities ..."

Ten

*Q: As one becomes more Spiritually Attuned, can one
expect life to become easier, more prosperous and less
demanding? Can one expect improved health, more
functional relationships and financial stability?*

A: Expectation is the product of single-minded drives
of the ego-self that condition mortal man to place time
limits, conditions of acceptance and performance
parameters upon the experience of assimilating The
Wisdom of One. How is it that the concerns of an
apparent earnest seeker of enlightenment would be
directed towards conditions of comfort and physical
well-being? How is it that a soul incarnate who would
seek the experience of Spiritual Attunement would also
seek short-cuts in the attainment of such or would be
preoccupied with finding easier, less demanding life-
conditions? How is it that a soul incarnate who would
choose to release self from the bonds of material
entrapments would nevertheless find great comfort
and security in that which he/she can see, hear, taste,
smell and touch?

To answer these questions mankind has need to understand that the Spiritual Path is not a road chosen to
facilitate the embellishment of self or to strengthen

one's personal interests in and control over third dimension reality; rather, the Spiritual Path is chosen to help mortal man learn how to become One with all Universal Realities; that is, the Spiritual Path is chosen to assist mortal man in learning how to exist in Harmony, Peace, Love and Fulfillment in The Light of One. Further, the Spiritual Path assists mortal man in gaining an understanding of his/her place within The God's Divine Order and allows mankind to experience the greater purpose of evolution from a more Universal perspective. No longer do the notions of personal well-being pervade thoughts and influence subsequent behaviors. No longer are there compelling concerns about the needs for personal survival. No longer does the world of material comfort seduce and delude consciousness, impairing judgement and compromising decision-making processes. Slowly mortal man comes to experience and accept the revelation that each soul incarnate being has chosen his/her life-conditions by which to learn The Lessons of Existence and that each soul incarnate being has or will have all that he/she requires (not necessarily all that he or she may want) to function effectively in his/her given reality. So you see, as one becomes more Spiritually Attuned, mortal man realizes that indeed he/she has much to be thankful for and that in Truth, all things do exist as One.

When a soul incarnate chooses to willingly surrender the conscious will of mortal man to The Greater Will of The Universal One, the varieties and amounts of mental and emotional stresses that can impact heavily upon mortal consciousness are significantly reduced, directly affecting the state of one's physical health. With the reduction of stress levels, one feels and becomes more alive, less encumbered by nagging, chronic pains and recurring illnesses. Additionally, when mortal man fully commits self to participating in the process of Spiritual Attunement, one's personal relationships naturally improve. Improved relationships are simply a function of one's improved perception of self, which allows a greater sense of Compassion and a deeper sense of Understanding to be executed when engaging life-circumstances or when interacting with the behaviors of one's brethren. Mortal man begins to look upon issues of self-importance and self-worth in ways that are more in keeping with the dynamics of Universal Law, as counterproductive behaviors are readily acknowledged and transmuted. Indeed, as one becomes more Spiritually Attuned, one's life-condition begins to blossom - not because one has "manifested goodness" or one has "willed" it to be so, but because one has "allowed" beneficent, fulfilling life-conditions to evolve by embracing self and The Unfoldment Process with Love, Compassion, Patience, Wisdom, Mercy and Serenity. One no longer acts with impatience, arrogance and anxiety, demanding attention and performance or seeking external sources for the validation and sanction of personal needs and choices.

It is also important to acknowledge that as mortal man becomes more Spiritually Attuned, the pitfalls and obstacles along the road toward enlightenment become more subtle and treacherous in design and function. It is that hostile, etheric factions are working to counter-balance the vibrations of Benevolence and Grace with vibrations of self-serving and discordant natures. This too is simply the natural order of third dimension reality. You see, as mankind moves closer to the moment of Harvest, there will be greater effort exerted by these hostile, etheric factions to direct mortal consciousness away from the fourth density state of "Christ-Consciousness" and toward the polarized state of fourth density consciousness that employs self-service as the motivation for existence. This invasive, compromising activity is designed to impair judgement and to color the experience of Spiritual Evolution with doubt. It is for each soul incarnate being to maintain focus and to adhere to The Truth of Spirit in The Light of One alive in his/her heart. This will allow one to negotiate the obstacles and pitfalls along the Path with the knowledge that to experience discordance serves to strengthen mankind's Conviction and Purpose, instead of impeding one's journey toward the assimilation of The Wisdom of One. It is for each soul incarnate being to engage his/her journey with the knowledge that each and every moment, every experience of physical life is important in awakening and reinforcing the evolution of self and only as the result of consciously choosing to engage all aspects of one's reality will the process of Spiritual Attunement facilitate the expression of the true God-illumined nature of mortal man.

"...Mortal man 'Heals' nothing; rather, one who engages in the Facilitation of Healing allows him/herself to be used as a Divine Catalyst for and acts as a humble participant in the Healing Process."

Eleven

Q: *What lessons must one learn or what initiations must one pass in order to become a successful Healer?*

A: It is by The Grace of The Creative Force of this Universe, THE INFINITE ONE, that all physical Healing functions occur. By virtue of the fact that mortal man can raise his/her resonance rate to tap into the energies of Universal Design does not mean that man can either control, or take credit for the resultant Healing that is Facilitated. Let us clearly understand that mortal man "Heals" nothing; rather, that one who engages in the Facilitation of Healing allows him/herself to be used as a Divine Catalyst for and acts as a humble participant in the Healing Process.

Frequently, we hear of those soul incarnates who have adopted the title "Healer" and in most every case such designations serve primarily to bolster egos and to falsely elevate the personal status of those so designated. In our view, participation in such self-aggrandizement, whether conscious or unconscious, is counterproductive and in some cases can prove harmful to both practitioner and client.

To become a successful facilitator, it is necessary to examine all aspects of self and to seek guidance, both intuitively and etherically, to transmute emotional traumas and wounds that perpetuate discordant thought and behavior patterns. Once the Intuitive Voice is accessed, then we find that etheric guidance is available to assist in the transformation process. The realizations that one makes regarding the nature and value of life, the perspective that one gains regarding the purpose and motivation for emotions and the obstacles that one engages and transcends along the path toward enlightenment serve as initiations and test one's Conviction and belief in The Wisdom of One.

"When mankind perceives reality through an open, evolved heart chakra, mortal man experiences reality by 'feeling' the energy states of that reality."

Twelve

Q: How does one learn to engage the heart chakra to "feel" reality, instead of perceiving reality through the conscious thought process?

A: Mortal man perceives that which he/she "thinks" to be reality through the conscious thought process, which is a process of speculation and testing that requires validation and/or documentation from some other outside source before the acceptance of fact or truth occurs. When mankind perceives reality through an open, evolved heart chakra, mortal man experiences reality by "feeling" the energy states of that reality. Further, due to the fact that one has chosen to be a participant in said experience by allowing self to "feel" the energies of that experience, the soul incarnate "knows" the true reality of the particular life-experience engaged - without need for qualification, reinforcement, approval or validation from anyone or from any third dimension authority.

When reality is engaged by the conscious thought process, all past experiences and conditioned thought patterns impact upon one's ability to clearly perceive the reality that one is experiencing. As a result of the limiting nature of the conscious mind, the Reality of Truth that one experiences is compromised, veiled or adversely impacted by subtle or dramatic elements of past experiences. Also, when one's reality is solely engaged by the conscious thought process, then one's perception of reality can be greatly influenced by past incarnate emotional energies that require identification and subsequent transmutation in order for the soul incarnate to continue the upward spiral of his/her evolutionary journey.

When we discuss "feeling" one's reality, we address the choice one makes to open his/her heart to all of the designs of mortal existence, without need or desire to hide or shield self from any reality, and the perceptions of truth that one is able to make through a sense of "knowingness" that is directly attributable to understanding and applying the elements of The Wisdom of One. This is not a process of blind faith that we address, mind you; rather, this Unfoldment Process allows one to embrace the God-self by trusting the voice of intuition, instead of trusting or following the perceptions made through the clouded, limited vision of conscious thought. When mankind chooses to access the wealth of knowledge available through heart-centered behavior and when mankind allows self to truly feel all that is experienced, then mortal man will have also chosen to exist within and express the reality of self through the evolved matrix of the heart chakra. It is then that mortal man will have chosen to exist in the state of God-self.

*"Fear is the specter
of uncertainty that
mortal man paints
with his/her own face.*

*...It is good and right
that mortal man
experience all
emotions,
the experience of fear
being no exception."*

Thirteen

Q: *Akhenaton, how do you define "Fear" and what can mortal man do to resolve Fear?*

A: Fear is the specter of uncertainty that mortal man paints with his/her own face. In effect, one learns to accept conditioned thoughts and counterproductive behaviors as one's Reality of Truth. Subsequently, mortal man is compelled to hide his/her eyes from the illusion of reality that has been created, as man's fears grow larger and more malevolent, causing man to run faster and faster to avoid the reality of his/her own distorted vibration.

You see, the experience of fear is a normal occurrence in human evolution, as lifetimes of conditioning have predisposed mortal consciousness to accept the imprint of fear. It is mankind's perpetuation and promulgation of misinformation, half-truth, myth and delusion that provides fertile soil within which fear takes root and grows. This we see as the established pattern, but man makes choices that sustain this pattern. Further, at each soul incarnate's time of readiness, he/she can choose to confront and transmute the fears that have caused counterproductive behavior patterns and achieve Karmic Resolution. It is at this point that the mortal incarnate begins to accept responsibility for the choices he/she has made and without adversely judging self, releases self from the cycle of anguish, guilt, repression and denial.

Nonetheless, it is good and right that mortal man experience all emotions, the experience of fear being no exception. Mankind is to experience firsthand, that is man is to feel on an intimate, personal level, the dynamics of all emotions. It is the experiencing of emotions that ultimately facilitates man's awakening to understand the egocentric motivations that underlie all discordant emotions.

"It is the function of Karma that allows mortal man to continually engage in discordant behaviors until he/she chooses to embrace the revelation of Truth - that all things born of Creation exist as One -"

Fourteen

Q: *What is "Karma" and how do you define "Grace"?*

A: Simply put, Karma is the law of retribution or the Universal Principle of cause and effect and Grace is the revelation of Truth that ultimately leads to the unfoldment of The Wisdom of One in the hearts and deeds of mortal man. You see, those behaviors that man perpetuates that are in opposition to Universal Law and Divine Will remain a part of the memory matrix of the soul and find expression in each successive incarnation until the mortal incarnate acknowledges and takes responsibility for his/her discordant behaviors, forgives all those associated with the discordant scenarios (including him/herself) and consciously chooses to change the thought patterns that allowed the counterproductive behaviors to occur.

It is the function of Karma that allows mortal man to continually engage in discordant behaviors until he/she chooses to embrace the revelation of Truth - that all things born of Creation exist as One. As a result of this moment of Grace, mortal man chooses to release him/herself from the reincarnate journey of discordance through Karmic Resolution and to ascend the evolutionary ladder of enlightenment toward becoming an Initiate of The Light of One.

"...One's personal connection to The Infinite Body of God cannot be shaken and will ultimately facilitate the unfoldment of Wisdom and Truth."

Fifteen

Q: *Akhenaton, how does one overcome failures in life and learn to master the drives and compulsions of ego?*

A: There is either understanding and acceptance in this life, or there is confusion and resistance. Either there is Conviction and faith, or there is uncertainty and disbelief. Either there is Patience and contentment, or there is restlessness and irritability. These statements address one's perception and treatment of his/her life-condition and further address the notion of mastery or mastership. In addressing life-conditions, mortal man masters nothing, as it is truly drives of ego that would compel mankind to seek conditions of perfection and it is the self-absorbed interests of arrogance that would compel mankind to proclaim the attainment of absolute states of existence.

It is when mortal man learns to accept life-conditions as being good and right for the evolution of self that man begins to become a willing participant in the continuum of life-experience. This allows mortal consciousness to comprehend at increasingly higher, more profound levels of Spiritual Truth that the meaning and purpose of mortal existence lies in man's ability to serve Creation and to allow all things to simply be.

Understanding and acceptance allow mankind to engage any life-condition without being compelled to impact upon or to create designs of change, as indeed all conditions find the appropriate moment of resolution when it is good and right to execute stages of transition. Conviction allows mankind to know that no matter what external factors may be in operation, one's personal connection to The Infinite Body of God cannot be shaken and will ultimately facilitate the unfoldment of Wisdom and Truth. Patience allows mankind to remain calm and to acknowledge the validity of all realities without being compelled to react to any situation or condition; rather, to flow with the current of life and to allow the reality of all things to be known and to exist in The Light of One.

"... Through the quietude of one's own heart-centered Meditation can one feel The Radiance and hear The Voice of God."

Sixteen

Q: *How does one know if he or she should attempt to become a Healing Facilitator?*

A: It has been said of The Spiritual Path and of the soul incarnates who serve the needs of Creation that there are those soul incarnates who choose such paths of righteousness and responsibility and indeed that there are those soul incarnates who are "chosen". Those who seek paths of enlightenment and choose roads of service willingly open their hearts to embrace the children of Creation with Love, Compassion and Mercy and through their personal commitment and unfoldment the knowledge and Conviction of Truth grow stronger, more radiant and more visible in their eyes and actions. It is through these earnest seekers that Divine Light Vibrations flow to illuminate the path of Soul Evolution and also through whom the facilitation of emotional and physical transformations can occur.

Conversely, those soul incarnates who are "chosen" are simply living out the expression of past incarnate knowledge and have accessed skills applied at former times under other life-conditions. It is interesting to note that many of those soul incarnates who are truly "chosen" are or have been faced with the choice of the Spiritual Path or the material world of third dimension at every stage of life. It is for those soul incarnates with heightened perceptions and abilities to seek the comfort and Truth of their own Intuitive Wisdom to find the answers, as through the quietude of one's own heart-centered Meditation can one feel The Radiance and hear The Voice of God.

To directly answer the question, *"How does one know if he or she should become a Healing Facilitator?"*, we would pose another question, *"How is it that one does not know?"* You see, facilitation can only be successfully engaged by soul incarnates who are willing to embrace the process of Birth/Integration/Rebirth/Integration/ Ascension for The Greater Good of all Creation. Where there is doubt, self-serving design or fear there cannot be an altruistic, confident soul vibration of Conviction capable of performing the often difficult, demanding task of Healing Facilitation. Where there is unresolved Karmic Debt that stimulates approach/avoidance behavior, an unwillingness or inability to fully commit to the life of Spirit or blatant denial of one's true life purpose, there cannot be totally successful Healing Facilitations. Only those who are able and willing to commit their minds, bodies and spirits to the needs of Creation, without compromising the Choice of Free Will of any mortal incarnate who would seek service, can be expected to become effective, conscionable Healing Facilitators.

"...That which is Truth will always be Truth and will always 'feel' good and right."

Seventeen

Q: How can a person learn to be more "Godly"?

A: Godliness is a natural function of human evolution. As mortal man discovers heart-centered behavior to be the most viable avenue toward the attainment of self-realization, more and more thoughts become filled with and subsequent behaviors motivated by Love, Compassion, Patience and Mercy. Again, it is through mortal man's conscionable application of Divine Truth that the consciousness of mankind moves closer to The Divine Conscience of The One.

To strive for what one "believes" to be a state of Godliness can be most misleading and counterproductive, for it is only the conscious mind acting through drives of ego that would urge one to consider or would compel one to embark upon such a quest. Striving toward conditions that one " believes" to be appropriate allows mental processes such as rationalization and/or intellectualization to greatly impact upon the decision-making process and subsequent behaviors. While analytical processes are valuable assets in man's negotiation of some third dimension realities, without the grace of Intuitive Wisdom, mortal man could not have evolved to the point where contentions of

Godliness are of any relevance at all.

To think is to engage the conscious mind, which requires validation through documentation and support systems to substantiate that which is believed to be truth. *To know* is to understand through reflection with the guidance of Intuitive Wisdom, wherein the soul incarnate who has engaged vibrations of Intuitive Wisdom through an open, evolved heart chakra knows the Reality of Truth without need of validation - because that which is Truth will always be Truth and will always "feel" good and right.

So you see, the notion of Godliness arises from those who observe others during the performance of benevolent tasks and services. Those who willingly and cheerfully perform such tasks or services are not engaged in said tasks for the purpose of *being Godly*; rather, these servants of Creation are engaged in benevolent acts because they know their behavior to be appropriate - to be good and right in The Eyes of The One. It is for the foregoing reasons that we say that Godliness is a natural function of human evolution, because the ultimate goal of mortal consciousness is to return to the wonder and grace that is The LoveLight Vibration of One.

*"... Only as a result
of following one's
heart-centered,
Intuitive Wisdom
in the service to
mankind can one
truly know what
behaviors are
appropriate."*

Eighteen

*Q: How can one be sure not to violate Universal Law
by compromising another person's Choice of Free Will?*

A: To compromise another soul incarnate being's
Choice of Free Will is to engage in any activity that
either actively or passively, consciously or unconsciously, with malice or through innocence serves to
manipulate, control or otherwise adversely influence
the course of another soul incarnate being's evolutionary journey. To engage in any behavior that would
impact upon another mortal being's journey of Soul
Evolution, without having been specifically asked by
that soul incarnate to answer direct questions, to assist
him/her or to facilitate a moment of awakening, vio-
lates the precept and order of Choice of Free Will.
Even when asked, it is conscionable to render only that
information which is specifically required to answer
said question, without offering personal commentary
or without engaging in the *"if I were you, I'd ..."* point of
view. To offer information beyond that which is necessary to answer any given question is not only counterproductive, but disregards the true need of other mortal beings as well.

Each soul incarnate being engages mortal life to discover his/her own truth of reality and in so doing, he/she can progress one step farther in the journey of Soul Evolution. Additionally, each mortal being has the undeniable, irrevocable right to choose those thought and behavior patterns that will best serve the needs of his/her evolution of self, even if said choices appear to an outside observer to be foolish, counterproductive, unnecessary or harmful. A mortal being who thinks that he/she knows better that which another soul incarnate should or must do to successfully negotiate reality is a mortal being who lives in egocentric delusion. You see, it is for each child of Creation to acknowledge and to allow all other children of Creation to experience life-events without judgement or interference, as well as to engage the moment of readiness for acceptance of higher truths at the pace that is good and right for each individual soul incarnate being. To be sure, it can only be good and right that choices are made to affect The Greater Good of all things born of Creation.

When man adopts behaviors that impact upon the Choice of Free Will of other soul incarnate beings, elements of Karmic Design are frequently engaged. What this means is that responsibilities for Karmic Debt can be shifted or transferred unwittingly from the energy matrix of one soul incarnate being to the energy matrix of another mortal incarnate. It is the direct result of intervention or encroachment upon the Karmic Path of another incarnate being, through misguided intent or through desire to influence, that allows for transference of Karmic Energy to occur. In effect, the soul incarnate who thinks that he/she is helping another soul incarnate by directing the thought and subsequent behavior patterns of that soul incarnate is in truth accepting elements of Karma from the one who was thought to have been helped. In such cases, neither party is effectively or conscionably served by the behaviors described.

One whose Karmic Energy has been accepted by another will continually find self confronted by the same types of troubling scenarios that he/she received assistance in temporarily or partially resolving. This is one of the applications of the Law of Karma that allows mortal man to stay in proximity to those energy states that will ultimately facilitate the learning of The Lessons of Existence. Further, the repeated cycle of discordant scenarios will remain in effect until the soul incarnate discovers the fundamental reasons underlying the discordant attitudes or hostile energy matrix shrouding him/her. However, it will now be more difficult to discover the reasons for his/her discordant life-condition, for the intervention by another soul incarnate being will have served to cloud and distort the true reality of the problematic life-situation. Conversely, the soul incarnate who would attempt to be of assistance by offering words and energies that he/she thinks will remedy the discordant situation frequently finds instances of bewildering confusion, emotional draining and a general sense of debilitation to be the rewards for compromising Choice of Free Will and accepting responsibility for another's Karmic Energy. Indeed, these can be some of the consequences for following the misguided, convoluted directives of the ego-self.

Many would seek further clarification of the nature and dynamics of Karma and Choice of Free Will by asking, *"How do Karma and Choice of Free Will apply to parent/child relationships? How does a parent raise a child, teaching him/her the rules of society, and not influence the child's Choice of Free Will?"* These are valid questions that upon examination reveal the simplistic nature of Karma and the linear function of Choice of Free Will.

You see, both parent and child make pre-incarnate, Karmic choices to engage each other in a given incarnation, so that both will be able to engage specific energy states or emotional interactions that will assist in the unfoldment of The Wisdom of One. It is through mutual consent at the soul-level that the different energy states or levels of consciousness of family members choose to assemble. As the result of the interactions of the various energy states within a family group, Karmic interactions as well as the potential for Karmic Resolution can be realized.

Once the parent has transmitted the parameters for acceptable social behavior to the child (usually by age seven the foundations for accepted societal conduct have been established), it is then the role of the parent to nurture and reinforce those behaviors that lead to conscionable, productive attitudes and life-conditions. Since both the parent and child will have consented to engage each other's vibrations as a part of their individual and mutual evolution of self, then there is no compromise of the child's Choice of Free Will by the parent who diligently directs the course of his/her child's behaviors. Further, it is solely the activity of the unrefined survival and pleasure drives of the child's ego-self that resist parental efforts of socialization.

As the child grows through adolescence and into young adulthood, it is for the parent to acknowledge the child's right to experience the vicissitudes of life, without attempting to shield, protect or otherwise direct the child away from the living participation in and experience of mortal existence. Though it is doubtful that many parents would consciously or willingly choose for their children to experience sadness, uncertainty, frustration, resentment and emotional or physical pain, it is nevertheless necessary that all soul incarnate beings have the opportunity of working through discordant emotions and problematic life-situations. It is through the engagement of discordant emotions and troubling life-conditions and the subsequent transmutation or resolution of these energies that mortal consciousness learns to appreciate The Greater Reality of The Universal One. It is at this level of interaction that many parents inadvertently compromise the child's Choice of Free Will, even though parental actions may have been born of genuine concern for the child's safety and well-being.

It is to understand that only by following one's heart-centered, Intuitive Wisdom in the service to mankind can one truly know and apply those behaviors that are appropriate and good and right, without encroaching upon or adversely influencing another soul incarnate's Choice of Free Will. It is through one's acknowledgement and application of Selflessness in the treatment of his/her brethren and all things born of Creation that one facilitates the awakening of Etheric Love and Divine Understanding. It is then that mortal man can embrace the purpose and need for Choice of Free Will with The Conviction and Conscience of The Universal One.

"...Balance between masculine/feminine or left brain/right brain energies is essential for evolution of consciousness."

Nineteen

Q: *In other texts, you have written about "The God" meaning The God Spirit and have given this All-Knowing Presence a masculine image. How is it that you chose to identify a masculine God Presence in some of your writings, but give little attention to the feminine Goddess Presence?*

A: To understand the character of the pervasive, omnipresent Energy of The God Spirit is to understand that the illusion of polarized masculine/feminine energy states is misleading, for these aspects of The God Spirit are energy states that actually exist as a continuum of balance within Universal Order. It was not and is never our intention to imply that The God Spirit is singularly a masculine entity, as indeed It is not. Nevertheless, as a result of conditioned thought patterns and erroneous assumptions made about our purpose and motivations, it is possible for some soul incarnates to misconstrue the issues we present and subsequently think that we would entertain sexist attitudes or arbitrarily assign a masculine, authoritative identity to The God Spirit. To believe such could not be farther from the truth.

In the allegorical format of "Creation's Promise", it was and is our intention to show a personified image of The

God Spirit that is all-encompassing: Father, Mother, Sister, Brother, Daughter, Son - each existing simultaneously within The God Consciousness, as indeed The Universal God-Head nurtures each of these states of being in the evolving consciousness of mortal man. Though we refer to The God as Father, we present The God Presence as being Benevolent and Merciful, filled with Determination and Tenderness, directed by Conscience and Insight, inspired by Compassion and Conviction, sustained by Patience and Wisdom and eternally renewed by Serenity and Love in The Light of One. Certainly such an image of The God Spirit is one that exemplifies balance and harmony, which clearly invalidates the notion that we would present The God Spirit as a singularly masculine presence or as driven or motivated solely by masculine energy. It has always been our position that balance between masculine/feminine or left brain/right brain energies is essential for evolution of consciousness, the extrapolation from which would identify The God Spirit as the very ideal or model of balance and harmony that mortal consciousness would seek to emulate.

It is for us at this writing as it has always been to identify The Yahweh Entity* as "The Father" of modern man and to identify the Earth as mankind's nurturing

* *Though we identify The Yahweh Entity as "The Father", we also acknowledge The Yahweh Entity as a social memory complex, which is the living consciousness of an entire civilization, the physical representation of which is seen in vision as a gentle, compassionate, youthful, androgynous Being of Divine Light Energy.*

100

Mother. Our references to Earth as, "the garden of life", "the garden of Creation" or as "the womb of mankind" in the text of "Creation's Promise" clearly substantiate our view and abiding respect for The Earth Mother. Further, by understanding and accepting that The Yahweh Entity as well as The Council of Twelve exist as Evolved Light Energy Consciousness States, we also acknowledge the presence of The Yahweh Entity and The Council of Twelve existing as One with The God Presence or functioning in harmony with Universal Conscience. Therefore, the personification of The God-Head as endowed with Strength and Gentleness, Understanding and Determination and Clarity of Perception and Joyful Wonderment are in keeping with Spiritual Traditions throughout the world that acknowledge the energy of life and consciousness as generated from one, central, Universal Source.

When we think of that which is The God Spirit, we envision and feel the Benevolence, the Grace and Conviction that is The Presence of The Infinite One. We experience the transcendence of the ego-self, thus releasing the need to debate whether it is right or wrong to address The God as The Father or The Mother. When we think of that which is The God Spirit, we allow self to simply exist within The Universal Love that has no polarizing elements - we simply allow self to enjoy existence within The Light of The One.

*"...Mortal conscious-
ness is not simply the
physical vessel that
houses the soul -
Mortal Consciousness
is the Soul, the living,
evolving matrix of the
heart chakra -
The God-self."*

Twenty

Q: Akhenaton, how does one successfully negotiate feelings of disappointment, anxiety or frustration?

A: One only experiences disappointment when and if he/she has come to anticipate some action, or level of performance, or receipt of some material gift that would enhance a given pleasure state or would contribute to the satisfaction of the ego-self. When one expects to receive something special or particularly pleasing, invariably on some level, one begins to savor the illusion of pleasure and self-importance long before the actual event takes place. It would then be understandable for there to be a period of discontent or a letdown following the anticipation and the subsequent disappointment of not receiving that which was anticipated would nurture, enhance or render comfort to the ego-self. Indeed it is anticipation that stimulates anxiety and frustration follows the disappointment of not having some anticipated state or condition of the ego-self fulfilled. However, it is only one's perception of self or rather one's perception that conditions of physical pleasure and emotional reinforcement are necessary for one to establish and maintain a positive image of self that creates a pattern of expectation/disappointment/frustration/depression, for to look outside of self for validation or justification for one's sense of self-worth can be both counterproductive and debilitating.

It is for each mortal incarnate to learn that one cannot predicate his/her reality upon that which is seen through another's eyes. Each soul incarnate's personal reality lives only in his/her true perception of self and validation for such comes as the result of the opening, clearing and evolution of the heart chakra. To be sure, it is for each mortal incarnate to understand that mortal consciousness is not simply the physical vessel that houses the soul - Mortal Consciousness is the Soul, the living, evolving matrix of the heart chakra - The God-self.

When mankind comes to observe reality from the vantage point of Spiritual Evolution, then human hearts will feel and know how transitory and unimportant drives and desires for pleasure and self-enhancement are; then mortal consciousness will allow the release of self from the influence of controlling emotions, but without having had the experience of disappointment, anxiety or frustration, how would mankind truly know such a release to be good and right? How can mortal man "know" anything if he/she doesn't experience the reality of life? If mortal man doesn't feel the emotions of the ego-self and choose to transcend that which is discovered to be unnecessary and counterproductive, then learning, the evolution of the God-self and Karmic Resolution cannot occur.

*"… To speak of
Spiritual Truth and
then to think and act
in ways that are in
contradiction to
the philosophy that
we teach would be
unconscionable."*

Twenty-One

Q: It is said that one day each week you voluntarily observe silence during the daylight hours, communicating only by means of gestures and handwritten notes. What is the purpose of this practice?

A: We engage the weekly day of silence to honor in quietude The Grace of Spirit and to nurture and embrace The Light of One alive within us. We engage the day of silence to help maintain and to cleanse the open heart chakra. Observance of silence also allows us the opportunity to identify and surrender any obscure, lingering compulsions of the ego-self to the patient, forgiving, everlasting Presence of Divine Will. This practice further allows us to focus upon the purity of the God-self through which we identify The Living Presence of The God Spirit.

Our conscious choice to observe silence is also the result of a deep sense of discipline and devotion to Spiritual Evolution that pervades every aspect of our life-condition. You see, to speak of Spiritual Truth and then to think and act in ways that are in contradiction to the philosophy that we teach would be unconscionable.

We can only be as we are, which means that we must represent that which lives within us with diligence, respect and sincerity.

In many Religious and Spiritual Traditions, the observance of silence for special periods of time is customary. In the observance of particular rites, or in the honoring of Divine Presence, or as an act of contrition, voluntary abstinence from speaking has its roots in ancient practices. Many Mystics, Ascetics and members of Eastern Cultures routinely engage in the observance of silence as a part of the process of becoming One with all things. Though we cannot speculate as to why one soul incarnate would choose to observe silence and another would not, it is enough to know that ultimately we each come to embrace behaviors that are good and right for all things born of Creation.

*"... We define the
God-self as a condition
of Spiritual Evolution
that reveals mankind's
innermost, evolved
consciousness to be
a state of inherent
Divine Truth."*

Twenty-Two

Q: Please explain the relationship between "Intuitive Wisdom" and the "God-self".

A: Just as we define Intuitive Wisdom as a condition of "inner-knowingness" born of past incarnate experience, so do we define the God-self as a condition of Spiritual Evolution that reveals mankind's innermost, evolved consciousness to be a state of inherent Divine Truth. It is the expression of the God-self that is Light-minded in activity and is the result of mortal man's conscious desire to transmute counterproductive, discordant behavior. As mankind allows self to evolve in The Light of One, the God-self emerges as man's true, heart-centered nature. Through Intuitive Wisdom mortal man negotiates the journey of Soul Evolution. Through the God-self mortal man expresses the results of Soul Evolution.

As mankind continues to assimilate the dynamics of The Wisdom of One, while acknowledging and utilizing the presence and guidance of Intuitive Wisdom and the God-self, too will mortal man recognize that in the journey toward enlightenment there is truly nothing to seek, but rather everything to accept; there is truly nothing to long for, but rather everything to allow;

there is truly nothing to demand of self or of anyone or anything else, but rather everything to embrace in the benevolent arms of Love. What this means is that as mankind allows the directives of the ego-self to become extinguished, mankind willingly allows the surrender of mortal consciousness to The Greater Conscious Will Of The One. It is through the God-self that The Conscious Will Of The One finds expression within third dimension and it is Intuitive Wisdom that facilitates the unfoldment of this Divine Process.

"…It is most frequently observed that disease and pain accompany the choice that a soul incarnate makes to engage aspects of consciousness that require transmutation."

Twenty-Three

Q: Akhenaton, can you explain why we as human beings contract diseases and experience suffering and physical pain?

A: It is not for this one to say why all mortal incarnates contract illness and disease or choose to experience physical, mental or emotional pain, for this is an answer that is best left to each individual soul incarnate to uncover through his or her personal evolution of consciousness. Certainly there are common factors that stimulate conditions of pain and disease or predispose one to experience such conditions, but it is not to say that each mortal incarnate will have the same reac tion under similar conditions.

In some cases, there is need to experience states of debilitation in order to transcend or to identify and release self from counterproductive behavior patterns; that is, there is need to engage the process of Karmic Resolution. In other cases, disease and pain may serve to facilitate learning through situations designed to teach mortal man how to strengthen Conviction in surmounting obstacles to the assimilation of The Wisdom of One. In still other cases, pain, disease and suffering may serve to dramatically communicate and to boldly ground the reality in mortal consciousness that mankind has the responsibility of attending Mother Earth and all Kingdoms upon Her with the Light-minded Ideals of Universal Law.

More specifically though, it is most frequently observed that disease and pain accompany the choice that a soul incarnate makes to engage aspects of consciousness that require transmutation, especially those aspects of consciousness that involve the retention, repression, denial or withdrawal from emotional situations and/or energies. Frequently, it is seen that due to arrested, confused or imbalanced emotional energies, physical pain or the predisposition to illness or disease results. It is then that man can look to behavior patterns of this and past incarnations to find clues that will lead to the understanding of choices of behaviors and subsequent episodes of disease or pain. It is when choices are made to accept realities as they are found that man learns to release self from the compulsions and drives of the ego-self, finally resolving Karmic Energies that will have followed one for countless generations.

"…It is a matter of intuitive comprehension and etheric validation that confirms the reality of having accessed various states of expanded consciousness."

Twenty-Four

Q: How does a person know if and when he or she has fully assimilated The Wisdom of One or has achieved the "God-illumined" state of consciousness?

A: If one must ask the question regarding the complete assimilation of The Wisdom of One, or seek validation for that which one believes to be advanced states of consciousness, then indeed one has not accessed the state of consciousness that he/she has attempted to access. Mind you, we speak neither with sarcasm, nor with arrogance; rather, we speak with absolute point of fact. When mortal man attempts to resonate with and assimilate spiraling levels of higher consciousness, it is a matter of intuitive comprehension and etheric validation that confirms the reality of having accessed various states of expanded consciousness. To be sure, the validation for every soul incarnate's evolutionary moment and subsequent transitions from one state of consciousness to the next is expressed and felt through the open heart chakra. One simply "knows" and trusts in The Wisdom of One as the basis for Understanding, Conviction and Truth.

But the anxious, persistent seeker would again ask, *"But really, how can I really know for sure? What feelings*

119

can I expect? What are the signs I should look for?" And again, as we have answered elsewhere, *"How is it that one does not know?"* You see, it is only the conscious mind acting out expressions of the ego-self that would first prompt these questions and subsequently direct one to continue to seek an answer that cannot be processed by the conscious mind, thereby invalidating that which could have been the reality of Spiritual Evolution. Invariably the conscious mind, under the directives of the ego-self, invades, pollutes and most often totally destroys the pure expression of Divine Truth revealed through the Intuitive Wisdom of the God-self.

When The Wisdom of One has become the Conviction of one's life-purpose and the God-illumined state of mortality shines through one's heart-centered expression of self, it is virtually impossible for all things born of Creation not to know on some level of consciousness that such a condition of Godliness is in evidence. It is virtually impossible not to see and feel the depth of Love, Serenity and Wisdom that radiate from such a blessed being who has allowed self to enter into a state of Oneness and Grace with The God Spirit. It is impossible that one such as this does not simply "know" The Truths of Existence and through the living reality of Divine Illumination light the path toward enlightenment for many other soul incarnates to follow.

"An Initiate of The
Light is one who
will have embraced
The Lessons of
Existence with
Courage, Conviction
and Love, sacrificing
self and personal
comforts for
The Greater Good
of The One ..."

Twenty-Five

Q: *Akhenaton, it is said that you are a "Fully Sealed Initiate of The Light of One". What does this designation mean?*

A: Sealing refers to the Etheric Process of opening, clearing, energizing and balancing the chakra vibrations, which in effect raises the mortal resonance pattern to more closely approximate the vibratory rate of The God Presence. Chakra Sealing* establishes the highest possible resonance rate that one can attain in any given incarnate state. One who is "Fully Sealed" can activate and balance all of his/her chakra energies and therefore balance vibrations of the body as the need arises.

This does not mean, however, that an Initiate of The Light of One is impervious to or unaffected by emotional discord. To the contrary, an Initiate chooses to feel all vibrations of life, even those vibrations that are painful. However, an Initiate of The Light of One can quickly regain balance and perspective by activating

---

* *See "Chakra Sealing & The Council of Twelve" in* Crystal Communion: LoveLight Meditations.

his/her Chakra Seals, especially when emotional conditions have caused a shifting or a draining of energies. Further, an Initiate knows that only by experiencing all aspects of emotional energy can true learning and the release of self from conditioned behaviors occur. In effect, the Initiate uses Chakra Seals to help resolve any lingering energies of emotional disconcert.

The Sealing Process can take just a few moments or may last several hours, much the same as episodes of Cosmic Illumination. Chakras may be Sealed one at a time on different occasions or several or all of the chakras can be Sealed in one session. (It should be noted here that there are a few Initiates who are authorized to engage in the Sealing of one or more chakras of the soul incarnates so designated as ready for the Sealing Process.)

An Initiate of The Light of One is a conscious soul vibration who has willingly and openly embraced the process of Soul Evolution. This is a soul initiate who will have engaged the deepest, darkest aspects of self and will have been successful in transmuting the counterproductive designs of Karma and the ego-self, thereby allowing the true expressions of the God-self to be his/her expression of reality. An Initiate of The Light is one who will have embraced The Lessons of Existence with Courage, Conviction and Love, sacrificing self and personal comforts for The Greater Good of The One and who functions to teach mankind and to conscionably apply The Wisdom of One to all things born of Creation.

When describing self, Initiates tend not to use or accept designations such as "Christed", "perfect being", or "realized master", for these terms can be misconstrued and point to aspects of the ego-self in operation proclaiming the attainment of ultimate degrees or absolute levels of competence. Indeed, Initiates do not think themselves to be perfect in the sense of being without mortal frailties and therefore better or superior to other soul incarnate beings; rather, Initiates look upon themselves and mortal life as a wondrous, ever-unfolding learning process that offers unlimited opportunities to become the very best Light-minded being that he or she can become. An Initiate of The Light of One has no need for such proclamations or designations, for to function as an Initiate is to transcend feelings and designs of self-importance and to engage mankind and all things born of Creation through an open, evolved heart chakra.

It is not unusual for an Initiate of The Light of One to have no conscious knowledge of his/her place and function in The God's Divine Order, but that by virtue of his/her behavior and the manner in which life is viewed and engaged, the imprint of Initiate is unmistakable in its absolute radiance of Divine Purpose. There are those who function as Initiates who will have engaged Etheric Initiations and will have thought said

Initiations to have simply been interesting or unusual dreams. This does happen with a relative degree of frequency, for it is totally unnecessary for some soul incarnates to consciously engage the process of Etheric Initiation, as the Intuitive self will comprehend the process and transmit pertinent information that the conscious mind will require to function efficiently. An Initiate of The Light of One is a soul incarnate who is at once and always a child of Creation who radiates with The Light, The Grace and The Presence of The Spirit of God and through whom other soul incarnates may touch, feel, see, hear and learn of the true Light-minded nature that is The Conscience of God alive in the body of mortal man.

"... There is a predominant sense that a state of knowingness has been activated that makes verbal communication unnecessary."

Twenty-Six

Q: What is the difference between "Cosmic Illumination" and the visionary sequences experienced in Meditation or during "Astral Projection"?

A: Cosmic Illumination is an intimate experience of Etheric Communion during which the illusion of time and space seem to be suspended, as the soul incarnate so engaged receives Etheric Transmissions that are designed to expand mortal consciousness. Episodes of Cosmic Illumination may last minutes or hours and in some cases, these instances of infusing mortal consciousness with information of galactic import can last for periods of days or even weeks. More often than not, instances of Cosmic Illumination are nonverbal, telepathic transmissions designed to awaken or to extrapolate upon intuitive knowledge regarding the order and operation of some aspect of Universal Function. Cosmic Illumination enables those incarnate beings who have tapped into areas of knowledge beyond third dimension reality to comprehend more detailed, dynamic constructs of Creation, enabling those who have chosen to accept such information to assist in the evolutionary process of mortal consciousness.

The primary difference between Cosmic Illumination and the visionary sequences of Meditation and Astral Projection is the nonverbal, telepathic mode of communication coupled with a state of limbo that literally freezes time. Third dimension reality is seemingly suspended and one experiences a sense of separation or detachment from the physical body. There can be verbal transmissions during instances of Cosmic Illumination as well, but there is a predominant sense that a state of knowingness has been activated that makes verbal communication unnecessary. Additionally, episodes of Cosmic Illumination leave one with profound understanding and an absolute sense of purpose that far and away surpass other visionary experiences. The only exception or experience of greater impact upon the consciousness of mortal man is the ultimate vision of the radiant presence of The Infinite One.

"It is the choice to employ reactionary behavior to express perceived reality that allows the emotions of the ego-self and linear thought processes to hamper the true experience and reality of life and self."

Twenty-Seven

Q: *Akhenaton, you have mentioned "Linear Thought Processes" and the manner in which the conscious mind works in association with the ego-self. Please elaborate upon Linear Thought Processes and explain the process by which the conscious mind can become an ally of the God-self.*

A: Processes or patterns of mortal thought can generally be described as one dimensional or linear, for mortal man attempts to follow and execute patterns of logic that either induce, or deduce answers to life's perceived mysteries and problems based upon that which one perceives or believes to have gone before or that which one perceives or anticipates will follow. Linear thought processes give birth to patterns of rationalization and intellectualization that frequently lead mortal man far away from the true reality of that which is experienced. Under the directives of the ego-self, the conscious mind will usually attempt to view and/or color life in a manner that is pleasing to self, or to portray self to the world as competent and able to control personal life-situations. Further, as the result of past conditioning, the conscious mind will generate thoughts and feelings of fear, doubt, anger, resentment, guilt, pain, sadness or hostility to confirm the ego-consciousness state of confusion regarding self-worth, personal validity and life-situations. As the result of such reactionary behavior patterns, the conscious mind engages illusions and delusions of self and distorts elements of reality. It is the choice to employ reactionary behavior to express perceived reality that allows the emotions of the ego-self and linear thought processes to hamper the true experience and reality of life and self.

Additionally, mortal man attempts to rationally explain Spiritual Constructs using a linear thought process to analyze the feasibility, application and purpose of Divine Truth. With its limited, egocentric nature, simple linear thought patterns cannot fathom the limitless nature and function of Divine Truth, as that which is Divine resonates at an energy level that continually renews itself; therefore, the beginning gives birth to new beginnings - the beginning is the end and the end is the beginning. Linear thought processes have difficulty accepting and explaining this point, because Divine Truth has few reference points within the reality of third dimension; that is, there are few concrete, physical references of Divine Truth that can be empirically studied to satisfy the linear process of mortal thought, as that which is Divine is born of Love, Etheric Truth and heart-centered Wisdom. Further, that which is born of Love is incongruent with subjective, analytical, egocentric processes of conditioned mortal thought. That which is Divine is validated by that which one feels as Truth in his/her open, evolved heart chakra, while that which is the product of linear thought requires documentation, validation and qualification from sources outside of self, before acceptance of an idea, opinion or hypothesized truth can occur.

It is not that we say that linear thought has no purpose or value, as in third dimension, indeed it has both; rather, it is that faulty, conditioned, subjective thoughts and reactionary reasoning processes can only aid the process of enlightenment by being acknowledged as counterproductive, then forgiven, blessed and finally transmuted. To be sure, all processes of thought and behavior are necessary and deemed to be good and right for different stages of Spiritual Unfoldment, for ultimately each evolving soul incarnate being will discover the appropriate avenues and tools that will facilitate unfoldment in The Light of One. In order to understand the shortcomings and limited nature of linear thought processes requires that one will have come upon the moment when he/she is willing to accept the limits of mortal potential and allow the limitless potential of Divine Consciousness to transform his/her expression of reality.

This is the moment when mortal man chooses to surrender the subjective will of mortal consciousness to The Greater Dynamic Will of The Universal One. This is the moment when mortal man chooses to release him/herself from the conditioned drives and compulsions of the ego-self. This is the moment when mortal man chooses to embrace The Wisdom of One.

As the result of the Unfoldment Process, the conscious mind readily becomes an ally of the God-self. When ego-consciousness has been significantly reduced or transmuted, the God-self gently directs the conscious mind to implement those attitudes and behaviors that are deemed appropriate, to be good and right through heart-centered, intuitive awareness and guidance. It is the implementation of God-illumined behaviors, participation in conscionable, selfless acts of service or under particular circumstances choosing not to act at all, thereby allowing all things to be, that indicate that the conscious mind is working in harmony with the God-self.

*"Karmic Resolution
allows mortal man
to truly embrace
the reality of self
and all things
born of Creation
in The Light of One,
unafraid and willing
to experience and to
accept all realities as
they are found -"*

Twenty-Eight

Q: Please discuss the process that you term "Karmic Resolution" and explain how one can be sure that behaviors associated with counterproductive patterns of Karma have been fully released.

A: Karmic Resolution is the process which each soul undergoes that allows mortal man to identify, accept and to break free from the bonds of societal conditioning that would perpetuate discordant, counterproductive behavior patterns. The dissonant, problematic behaviors of which we speak are seen in operation and move relatively unchanged from one incarnation to another. Karmic Resolution allows mortal man to free him/herself from feelings of guilt, feelings that would impugn or compromise a positive sense of self-worth and feelings that would engage illusionary or delusionary belief systems. Karmic Resolution allows mortal man to truly embrace the reality of self and all things born of Creation in The Light of One, unafraid and willing to experience and to accept all realities as they are found - not as one might wish them to be. Karmic Resolution offers mankind yet another tool, another key to unlocking the storehouse of mortal consciousness that holds the knowledge and the memories of The Wisdom of One.

As mortal man chooses to release self from counterproductive thought/behavior patterns and chooses to accept and to apply the principles of Divine Truth, so does mortal man engage the natural process of Karmic Resolution. You see, it is the intuitive and/or conscious drive of each soul incarnate to eventually become the very best, most evolved, most God-illumined being that he/she can become. To access this state of consciousness, thoughts and behaviors of counterproductive or discordant natures must be addressed and transmuted. This process is well known to most Spiritual Traditions throughout the world, but Karmic Resolution has become more of a conscious effort on the part of many, many soul incarnates outside of the sanctions and the teachings of formal Spiritual Traditions. As mortal man chooses to embrace more Light-minded thoughts and behaviors, there is less energy directed toward behaviors of discordance, the result of which allows mortal man to extinguish the need to engage in subsequent discordant behaviors in order to learn The Lessons of Existence.

Resolution of Karma or Karmic Debt is complete when and if scenarios of discordance that once caused pain or reactionary behavior no longer impact upon one's well-being or sense of self-worth. Generally, one is aware that Karma has been fully exhausted/released when one views discordant scenarios and remembers past behaviors, but no longer is compelled to repeat past, counterproductive behaviors. In effect, when

Karmic Resolution has been achieved, the soul incarnate views familiar discordant scenarios and simply smiles, thinking, *"Ah, now I understand."*

*"...Mankind has
an immediate need
to learn to look
beyond the moment
of physical life
to embrace The Reality
of Eternal Life."*

Twenty-Nine

Q: Can you comment about the feelings of "Grief and Sorrow" that surround the loss of a loved one?

A: Grief and sorrow usually address man's sense of personal loss or injury. Once again, it is the ego-self that is in operation, expressing a moment of sadness, of loss and emotional pain. Through the tears of sorrow and loss, through the feelings of emptiness and isolation, through the numbness of grief, the ego-self expresses moments of emotional pain associated with one's sense of connection to another mortal vibration. Under conditions of grief and sorrow, the ego-self expresses confusion and pain associated with one's sense of mortality, or one's illusions about the longevity of physical life or the finality of physical death, or frequently, one's delusion regarding the justice or what appears to be the state of injustice of Earthly existence.

When we discuss emotions such as grief and sorrow, we are discussing activities of the ego-self and expressions of discontent, for the God-self understands the "higher processes" in operation and accepts the need for the release from the physical plane as a natural progression. This does not mean, however, that the ego-self is engaged in perpetrating self-serving activities;

rather, that the ego-self is engaged in lower vibratory activities that are a necessary experience of third dimension reality. Having experienced the disquieting feelings of grief and sorrow allows the ego-self to slowly evolve to the point where the release of self from the need for such debilitating emotions can and will occur as the result of conscious choice.

Concurrently, the emergence of aspects of the God-self serves to reinforce this process of release and further facilitates the forgiveness and acceptance of self. It is for each mortal being to know that the time will come for all children of Creation to learn to release self from physical attachments of all kinds, choosing no longer to attempt to possess anyone or anything; rather, choosing to exist in a state of Harmony with and expressing Altruistic Love and Compassion, Patience and Mercy, words of Wisdom and blessings of Serenity for all things born of Creation.

Do understand that we do not take lightly the painfully real feelings associated with the grief and sorrow surrounding the loss of a loved one. We would, however, point out that mankind has an immediate need to learn to look beyond the moment of physical life to embrace The Reality of Eternal Life.

Public as well as private expressions of grief and sorrow do nothing to assist the soul incarnate who has disconnected; rather, prolonged periods of grieving frequently impede the disconnected soul incarnate's intra-dimensional progression. If indeed mortal man cares about other soul incarnate beings, then let mankind treat one another with Love and Compassion, Dignity and Mercy, Patience and Understanding while the opportunity exists to do so in physical life. Then may mankind come to know the blessings of Altruistic Love, Harmony and Grace; then may mankind come to know how to walk hand-in-hand upon Mother Earth in Peace; then will mankind know The Blessing of Eternal Love in The Light of One; then will mankind know mortal man to be the God-illumined Light-beings that mankind was created to be.

"Each day that we are given allows us to know greater, more dynamic communion with The God Spirit alive in all things born of Creation."

Thirty

Q: It is said that you do not celebrate birthdays or observe any Religious or traditional holidays, Akhenaton. Why is this so?

A: We have chosen neither to celebrate, nor to acknowledge any one day as being more important or any more significant in life than any other. Each day that we draw breath is a gift, a blessing, and we give thanks for and pay homage to The Spirit of One for the opportunity to learn more about this reality of physical life. Each day that we are given allows us to know greater, more dynamic communion with The God Spirit alive in all things born of Creation. We choose to embrace each day as if it were our last day of physical consciousness, for in so doing, the experience of life becomes an intimate experience of Respect, Integrity, Love, Harmony and Peace that we share with all of our brethren from the various Kingdoms upon Mother Earth.

Birthdays and traditional western holidays have become increasingly commercial and frequently serve to stimulate anxiety, frustration and states of depression - all of which are the products of conditioned, reactionary behaviors of the ego-self. Even the annual celebration of "Thanksgiving" can prove to be a disturbing experience for many soul incarnates. During this time of family gathering, the acts of dominance, manipulation and control that are so evident in many family units are once again displayed and the resultant reactionary, conditioned behaviors associated therewith are amplified and reinforced. Conversely, in the absence of a family unit, the feelings of loneliness, isolation, depression or the longing for physical contact with family members who are no longer on the physical plane can overwhelm mortal consciousness, compelling mortal man to engage in self-indulgent, self-destructive behaviors that impede the journey of Soul Evolution.

Within the nuclear family, sometimes the seeds of self-importance are unwittingly planted, as the child is conditioned to look forward to holidays, those special days throughout the year when he/she will receive gifts. It is not that we find feeling good about self to be counterproductive; rather, that to anticipate and to expect to be "stroked", or to be treated as a "special person", or to be lavished with gifts reinforces the illusion of the ego-self as being important. And the inevitable result of such thought and behavior processes is a letdown or a sense of disappointment that can be quite damaging to the illusion of self when expectations are not met. Further, it is not unusual for anxiety, depression and a growing sense of devaluation of self to develop when or if monetary considerations prevent one from purchasing that "special gift" for that "special someone".

If mankind has need to graphically demonstrate feelings of tenderness and personal connection with other soul incarnates, then is not it good and right to demonstrate such feelings each and every day of life? Is not it good and right to give back to life the same Love, Compassion, Mercy and Grace that await discovery by each incarnate being each and every day of life? To these questions we answer, "Yes, if indeed it is good and right, then let it be done with fervor and Conviction in The Light of One."

"Unconditional Love is a Divine State of Consciousness in which the virtues of the God-self are seen in full blossom."

Thirty-One

Q: Please explain the level of consciousness called "Unconditional Love".

A: Unconditional Love is not an aspect of emotion; rather, it is an enlightened state of consciousness, an evolved condition of Etheric Consciousness expressed in third dimension. Unconditional Love is a Divine State of Consciousness in which the virtues of the God-self are seen in full blossom. It is a state of being in which the evolved energy matrix of heart-centered consciousness merges with The God Spirit alive in all things born of Creation. For a soul incarnate being to experience the revelation of Unconditional Love, he/she will have had to engage all aspects of self and will have consciously and willingly chosen to actively and fully release the energies of the ego-self, thereby allowing self to experience the God-illumined state of Selflessness.

Unconditional Love is the altruistic state of consciousness in which the fully evolved energies of the God-self are one's personal expression of reality. Unconditional Love is the state of being in which mortal man's evolution to assimilate The Wisdom of One finds its moment of completion. Unconditional Love is the state of

Divine Consciousness in which mortal man finds his/her moment of ascended union with The Infinite Body of God.

*"The Beyond-
Consciousness is
a state of union
with the Akasha,
as well as a state
of communion with
The Universal
God-Head."*

Thirty-Two

Q: What is the state of being that you term "The Beyond-Consciousness"?

A: The Beyond-Consciousness is a state of evolution in which mortal consciousness and linear thought patterns have been surrendered (transformed) to The Greater Will of The Universal One. When man ascends to The Beyond-Consciousness, the ego-self and Karmic Debt have been resolved and the conscious being of mortal man has been elevated through fourth density ascension to accept and to apply the reality of The Wisdom of One to all life-situations and to all things born of Universal Creation. The Beyond-Consciousness is a state of union with the Akasha,* as well as a state of communion with The Universal God-Head.

It is not possible for the conscious mind to fathom the reality of The Beyond-Consciousness while shackled with fears, desires, the illusion of personal need and self-serving devices. It is when the consciousness of man evolves to appreciate the nature and function of

For additional information about The Akasha, see Question & Answer 49 of this text and refer to <u>Crystal Communion: LoveLight Meditations</u> under "Rhythmic Breathing".

the God-self that the possibility of comprehending the wonderment and Grace of The Beyond-Consciousness begins.

Further, it is not that we identify The Beyond-Consciousness as a state of God-Intoxication that generates a state of isolation, self-deprivation and withdrawal from participation in the experience of life; rather, that The Beyond-Consciousness facilitates a complete integration of Divine Truth with third dimension reality, allowing man to be of immeasurable service to his/her brethren. It is an absolute state of God-illumination that allows mortal man to resonate with and selflessly apply the precepts of Universal Law to all things born of Creation, thereby addressing the Reality of Truth that is "Beyond" the elements of existence that other soul incarnate beings are able to identify or validate as constructive. Additionally, as one engages aspects of The Beyond-Consciousness, one discovers the absolute simplicity with which life is designed and can be conducted, for no longer do the whims and demands of ego-consciousness impact upon decision-making and behaviors or compel emotional states of discordance.

As one becomes totally absorbed by the Knowingness, Peace and Grace of The Beyond-Consciousness, one aligns his/her energy matrix with the resonance of The Universal Mind, The Creative Thought Process that spawns all things born of Universal Creation. This is the ultimate moment of mortal awakening, as the vision of The Infinite One becomes more dynamic, increasingly clear, generating pulsating, warm, tingling sensations of cosmic expansion throughout the heart, third eye and crown chakras. This is the moment when mortal man no longer has questions. This is a time when a deep, abiding sense of understanding beyond understanding pervades mortal being. This is the moment when mortal man truly knows that indeed All Things Are As One.

*"... Soul incarnates
who engage in acts
of manifestation
most certainly
find self engaging
the cause and effect
application of Karma."*

Thirty-Three

Q: How does The Law of Karma apply to one's attempts at "manifestation"?

A: To manifest is to alter the natural course or to change or to influence the pattern of the Unfoldment Process of life-events. Soul incarnates who engage in acts of manifestation most certainly find self engaging the cause and effect application of Karma. It is not that planning for the future or that working toward a goal is an act of manifestation; rather, that to manipulate the nature or the unfoldment of life-events through ritual or by conscious action for self-serving reasons creates a cause and effect scenario that will require balance or retribution according to the dynamics of Universal Order. When one sets out to acquire or to achieve something with the single-minded drive to embellish self, then the mere thought of such an act, whether the act is successful or not, creates a mind-set that predisposes one to subsequent self-serving behavior patterns that will require attention and transmutation in this or some future physical incarnation. Acts of manifestation are neither acts of pragmatism, nor can they be justified through the conscience of the God-self.

You see, each physical incarnation is designed to afford

the soul incarnate the opportunity to evolve one or more steps closer toward the assimilation of The Wisdom of One. If during the course of an incarnation the conscious mind becomes compelled or seduced into engaging in acts of manifestation, this too will have been by predetermined design for the purpose of assisting the soul incarnate in comprehending some aspect of The Lessons of Existence. Further, by allowing self to engage behaviors that might be deemed counterproductive, the soul incarnate slowly comes to accept the reality that he/she might be better suited to engage in other types of behaviors, thereby releasing self from further need to engage discordance and allowing the counterproductive behaviors to fade into extinction.

During the past several years, we have seen many books and metaphysical workshops advertised using statements such as, *"Manifest your destiny!"* or *"Prosperity can be yours. Manifest your highest potential!"* or *"Have the job, the relationship and the comforts you want. Manifest your reality!"* Statements like these entice thousands of soul incarnates each year into displaying more exaggerated aspects of the ego-self by encouraging and promoting self-aggrandizement states. Many such books and workshops have taken the sound principle of establishing a positive sense of self-worth and have crossed the line into directing mankind toward states of self-importance. Clearly, notions of self-importance serve only to establish and to perpetuate Karmic Patterns of discordance.

Every mortal being wants happiness and comfort, financial security and fulfilling relationships, but at what cost? When the evolution of the God-self is consciously and willingly abandoned or through delusionary behaviors the God-self is denied for the sake of fleeting moments of physical contentment, then too the soul incarnate will have chosen to experience counterproductive behaviors that will ultimately require transmutation. Additionally, one can be sure that he/she will continue to encounter similar situations and similar discordant energies of self-serving natures until one learns the lessons connected therewith and develops the sense of Conviction to see beyond the compelling, sometimes overwhelming desire for physical or personal gratification.

"It is the Intuitive
Voice that speaks
softly and simply
waits for mortal man
to discover
The Wisdom,
Beauty and The Divine
Purpose of Truth."

Thirty-Four

Q: Akhenaton, how can one be sure that the "Intuitive Voice" is speaking and not simply the conscious mind acting to accommodate the ego-self?

A: The Intuitive Voice is gentle, calm and speaks with unmistakable clarity to the receptive ear/heart, as it guides mortal man or imparts information born of Absolute Truth. The Intuitive Voice never makes demands or issues admonitions, for such actions are directly attributable to the emotional matrix of the ego-self that holds energies of impatience, anxiety, uncertainty, fear, resentment and anger. The Intuitive Voice embraces mortal consciousness with Love, Compassion, Patience and Understanding without need to prove anything, without compelling urgency or need to dominate the process of being. It is the Intuitive Voice that speaks softly and simply waits for mortal man to discover The Wisdom, Beauty and The Divine Purpose of Truth.

Frequently, one may think that he/she is responding to the Intuitive Voice, but in fact may be responding to the secondary activity of the conscious mind that follows many expressions of the Intuitive Voice. What this means is that Absolute Truth may be offered for con-

163

scious expression by the Intuitive Voice and in the blink of an eye, the conscious mind will have begun asking questions, making judgements, seeking qualifications, analyzing or denying the moment of Absolute Truth that will have taken place. In effect, the moment of Absolute Truth is dissected, compromised, invalidated or destroyed by the conscious activities designed to protect, maintain or develop the illusions of the ego-self. This is the conditioning process of mortal consciousness in operation, working to inhibit the evolution of the God-self.

To be sure, the Intuitive Voice speaks through the heart chakra and each soul incarnate who experiences the Intuitive Voice in operation also experiences the knowingness of "feeling" the expressions of the Intuitive Voice. It is that one simply "knows" or recognizes words of Absolute Truth when such words are given. At the instant of transmission and reception of energies from the Intuitive Voice, warm sensations fill the heart chakra with Love and Understanding that allow mortal man to be at Peace with the energies transmitted. One simply "knows" when he/she has experienced Truth from the Intuitive Voice by the kind of comforting sensations that fill the heart, as well as vibrations that ground a sense of willingness to accept self and all aspects of consciousness without need for outside validation.

Indeed, this Process is one of Unfoldment, for it takes

time and Patience to learn how to differentiate between the energies of the Intuitive Voice and the often subtle, veiled activities of the conscious mind and the ego-self. It is a Process of Unfoldment, a Divine Process of Unfoldment, for the end result is not only Understanding through acceptance of Absolute Truth, but also through this Process of Unfoldment mortal man nurtures and watches the evolution and the emergence of the God-self.

"... Thoughts of 'superiority' over ... (man's) Earthly relatives was fostered by means of ongoing telepathic communications from etheric factions of hostility ..."

Thirty-Five

Q: What is the origin of man's thoughts of self-importance and egocentric behaviors? How did these attitudes and subsequent behaviors become ingrained in mortal consciousness?

A: Over 200,000 years ago, modern man was created through the processes of selective breeding and telepathic reinforcement. Utilizing the gene-pool from Homo sapiens sapiens and the incarnate form of The Yahweh Entity*, along with guidance from and conscious/unconscious telepathic communications with The Yahweh Entity, modern man was given physical form and substantial intellect with which to engage the reality of third dimension existence. Modern man, Homo sapiens, was a being of agility and keen senses. These attributes enabled him/her to more efficiently negotiate the situations of daily life. Additionally, modern man's more evolved intellect made it possible for him/her to develop complex social systems that far exceeded the functional practicality of the simple colonies and basic family groups of his/her predecessors.

---

* *For more information concerning The Yahweh Entity, refer to* <u>Discussions of Spiritual Attunement & Soul Evolution, Volume I</u>, *pages 8-9.*

During the early stages of modern man's emergence onto the face of Mother Earth, it was dramatically obvious that he/she was a much improved life-form, when compared to his/her close relatives, Homo sapiens sapiens and Cro-Magnon man, both of whom also populated Mother Earth at that time. It was during this early era of modern man's existence that thoughts of "superiority" over his/her Earthly relatives were fostered by means of ongoing telepathic communications from etheric factions of hostility, those galactic vibrations who opposed The Yahweh Entity and The Council of Twelve. Slowly, the thought of modern man's "superior nature" when compared to his/her Earthly relatives became an integral part of mortal consciousness. Soon thereafter Homo sapien began to exalt him/herself, raising personal status above other mortal beings deemed to be weaker, less efficient or inferior to him/herself.

These reinforced notions of self-importance in association with modern man's innate survival instincts gave birth to the ego-self. It was through the ego-self that modern man was then compelled to create social orders in which the establishment and the maintenance of the illusion of self (self-importance) was an active priority. You see, were it not for the intervention of hostile etheric energies, modern man could have possibly evolved displaying only those Light-minded Ideals represented by The Yahweh Entity and The Council of Twelve. Since this was not the case, it was inevitable that the lower, survival functions of mortal consciousness would be displayed in self-serving behavior and that the early expression of modern man's reality of self would reflect the pervasive influence of egocentricity.

Fortunately, the initial creative programming provided by The Yahweh Entity was not extinguished by the ego-self of modern man. However, the drives of the ego-self were so demanding, so absolutely compelling, that modern man could not perceive the gentle Truth of the God-self, as it attempted to guide modern man's activities toward more altruistic, benevolent behaviors. Nonetheless, the God-self, which was a part of the initial creative programming, remained alive but subdued within the consciousness of modern man and patiently awaited the time when it would receive viable expression.

"Judging is an active, compelling behavior . . . directed by the ego-self . . . acknowledging is a passive, reflective behavior that stimulates Understanding and Grace . . ."

Thirty-Six

Q: *Akhenaton, please explain your usage of the terms "Acknowledging" and "Judging" as they pertain to encountering the elements of one's reality or life-condition. Why is it important to understand the difference in application between these two terms?*

A: When a soul incarnate *acknowledges* an element of reality, he/she simply endeavors to identify the vibratory function, energy presence or orientation of that particular element of reality and allows it to be precisely that which it is, without need or compulsion to impact upon or to react to the state at which the life-condition or factor is discovered to resonate. One allows self to realize the unfettered, uncompromised truth of the experience of reality and accepts that which is as one finds it to be. Each soul incarnate being is then better able to accurately determine the nature and dynamics of his/her Reality of Truth, which is the individual, Universal expression of that which is the soul essence, as well as the Karmic Elements associated with each incarnate being. One will have conscionably engaged and accepted all things in the moment of Absolute Existence, for one will have focused and grounded his/her consciousness in The Truth of The Wisdom of One.

Conversely, when a soul incarnate attempts to *judge* the factors that comprise his/her reality, then he/she is seeking to categorize each experience and element of life in accordance with varying degrees of benevolence or discordance or as existing in a neutral state that poses no threat of discrediting the illusions of the ego-self. When one *judges* the elements of life, one reacts through conditioned thoughts and behaviors to that which is perceived as wrong or potentially harmful or thought to be right, beneficial or to offer the promise of pleasure, personal advancement or material gain. When a soul incarnate being engages in *judging* life-conditions or factors of reality, he/she invariably views life as being the experience of polarized thoughts, emotions, behaviors and events. Further, he/she assumes that the conscious mind is capable of controlling or successfully avoiding the effects of negative energy states, while simultaneously seeking those conditions thought to be benevolent - thus perpetuating the cosmic illusion of duality.

When one chooses to *acknowledge* aspects of reality, one also chooses to engage elements of life through evolved perceptions of conscience that implement Patience, Compassion, Wisdom, Mercy, Serenity and Altruistic Love in The Light of One as tools to assist in the identification and comprehension of all that one experiences in mortal life. Accordingly, one will have evolved through Light-minded Conscience to accept the proposition that all life-conditions are to be embraced with The Precepts of Divine Truth and Universal Love, for in so doing, one impacts The

Greater Good of all things born of Creation through conscionable acts of service and by engaging behaviors designed to initiate and sustain Love, Peace and Harmony. *Acknowledging* one's reality facilitates a sincere, fulfilling state of understanding that reveals Selflessness to be the foundation upon which perceptions of truth are based. This allows one to experience all aspects of mortal life without need for personal protection from perceived threats of hostility and discordance, as well as granting one an unparalleled depth of understanding of the nature, dynamics and function of any life-condition engaged. Further, it is found that when one removes the importance of self from any scenario, then one can see the truth of that which is, instead of indulging self with concerns of possible adverse effects, short-comings or potential dangers that any element of life-experience might conceivably precipitate.

When one chooses to *judge* life-situations, one also chooses (consciously or unconsciously) to allow past fears, anxieties, frustrations, angers, resentments, hostilities, confusions and the immediacy of self-interest to impact upon perception, thereby influencing the course of one's subsequent behavior. In effect, *judging* aspects of life-experiences clouds mortal consciousness with both realized and imperceptible elements of discordant memories and energies of hostility. It is then that one is compelled to react to life-situations to protect one's sense of well-being or to preserve one's illusion of self. Additionally, *judging* stimulates reactionary behavior patterns that result from one's uncertainty of personal status or ability to effectively negotiate a perceived discordant life-experience. Similarly, it is the uncertainty of one's personal Reality of Truth that stimulates anxiety, fear and hostility, serving to perpetuate *judgemental*, reactionary behaviors when one is confronted by new, unfamiliar or potentially problematic life-situations.

Understandably though, differentiating between *acknowledging* and *judging* life-experiences can initially seem confusing, as societal conditioning and standards for "acceptable behavior" will have implanted and nurtured patterns of *judgemental* thought and behavior in the conscious mind of man - which is yet another factor that stimulates and maintains ego-consciousness. Another element that can complicate the acceptance and impede the implementation of the *acknowledgement* process is the experience of emotional conflict, confusion and distress associated with one's conscious attempts to engage life-situations without *judgemental* attitudes. Due to the fact that emotional imprinting is a learned behavior, as well as the product of Karmic Debt, it is necessary for mortal man to accept the premise that the experience of emotional trauma is neither a punishment for errors in decision-making, nor is it punishment for failures in the execution of life-tasks. Further, the experience of emotional trauma is not a signal that one is delving into inappropriate aspects of mortal life; rather, that emotional trauma serves as an important reference point or road-sign alerting one that a vital Lesson of Existence is being engaged. It is the task and ultimate responsibility of each soul incarnate being to accurately determine the nature of each lesson engaged and to conscionably apply that which is learned toward The Greater Good of all things. It is for each soul incarnate being to find the Strength of Conviction in his/her own heart-centered consciousness to rise above the overwhelming impact that fear and uncertainty associated with emotional discord can have and learn to embrace fear, uncertainty and emotional trauma in arms of Patience, Compassion, Mercy and Selfless Love.

In its simplest form, *judging* is an active, compelling behavior that initiates reactive, emotionally charged behavior in response to the experience of mortal life. The act of *judging* is a behavior directed by the ego-self that serves to isolate and limit one's ability to interact with life-conditions beyond the parameters of one's illusion of self and personal reality. *Acknowledging* reality is just the opposite, for *acknowledging* is a passive, reflective behavior that stimulates Understanding and Grace, which allows one to be at Peace when confronted by apparent hostility or adversity. It is through the *acknowledgment* of reality that one learns to access the greater moments of Peace and Contentment alive within the God-self. It is through the *acknowledgment* of reality that one can clearly perceive The Divine Purpose underlying all life-experiences. It is through the *acknowledgment* of reality that one learns to free self from the shackles of Karmic Debt to become a true, conscionable servant to the needs of Creation. The following example will illustrate the difference between *acknowledging* and *judging* life-conditions:

175

A soul incarnate being reports to work on Monday morning and finds a statement of employment termination on his/her desk. Prior to this time, there had neither been indications that the soul incarnate's job performance was in question, nor had there been significant personality clashes between the terminated soul incarnate and his/her co-workers or supervisors during the soul incarnates fifteen year employment tenure. If this soul incarnate has been conditioned to *judge* elements of his/her life-condition, then a probable behavior pattern that might be observed is as follows: Upon reading the termination notice, the soul incarnate might become consumed by bewilderment, astonishment and a sense of personal devaluation, the sense of unworthiness and embarrassment that one experiences when one is singled out as deficient, less capable or less intelligent than one thought self to be. For an instant, one might feel paralyzed, unable to think, speak or move, because to the conscious mind, the termination notice was both unexpected and unwarranted. Then the soul incarnate might seek an explanation for his/her termination from an administrator, but the soul incarnate will already be filled with emotional discord and concerns for immediate and long-term survival needs (even though survival concerns might only be fleeting thoughts amid the growing confusion and unrest in the soul incarnate's mind). The soul incarnate finds his/her supervisor and confronts the supervisor for an explanation for the termination notice. The supervisor shrugs his/her shoulders and says, *"I'm sorry, but it's out of my hands and there's no one else to talk to about it."* Then the supervisor turns and walks away. The soul incarnate is left with a feeling of helplessness, betrayal, abandonment and resentment toward the company administrators. Additionally, a sense of troubling uncertainty begins to stimulate a general, unspecified fear as to that which tomorrow might bring.

This behavior pattern illustrates the kind of reactionary behaviors that are generated through ego-consciousness and one's illusion of personal well-being. As can well be imagined, there are many other possible reactionary behaviors that this scenario could precipitate that range from violent verbal/physical confrontations initiated by the terminated soul incarnate to the soul incarnate making a silent, apparently uneventful departure from the company, while suppressing the emotions and feelings of resentment and mistreatment. It is important to understand that *judging* life-situations can only lead to reactionary behavior patterns, hostility and discordance, no matter whether the dissonant energy is graphically displayed to the world or whether energies of discordance are locked away within one's consciousness. In either case, one becomes an unwitting participant in the flow of inflammatory, hostile energies. Ultimately, hostility breeds hostility and further perpetuates reactionary behavior patterns that are designed to protect and maintain the illusion of the ego-self.

If one *acknowledges* aspects of his/her reality, then during this scenario of job termination, a very different movement of energy would occur. Upon seeing the notice of termination, the soul incarnate would seat him/herself, focus and ground his/her energies and offer a silent prayer for guidance. The soul incarnate who is *acknowledging* the reality of this difficult third dimension experience would most certainly feel the impact of emotional discord rising in him/her, but would neither suppress the energy by denying or detaching from the feelings, nor would he/she lash out in anger and frustration, demanding explanations, justice and respect. This soul incarnate would intuitively and consciously know that there was a Greater Purpose in operation, one that might not be readily detectable by the soul incarnate at that particular moment. Nevertheless, he/she would have faith in The Universal One that the change in life-course would have been designed to effect evolution of consciousness and at a time that was good and right the soul incarnate would have access to consciously understanding the reasons that the change in life-condition was appropriate.

It is this deeper commitment to The Truth of The Wisdom of One that allows the soul incarnate to feel the emotional energy surrounding his/her job termination without being compelled to react to that which might appear to be an attempt to discredit one's intelligence, capabilities or sense of well-being - as in truth, no mortal being can create a lasting, positive self-image for another mortal being, nor can it be taken away. One who is *acknowledging* reality allows self to feel all emotions and chooses to bless, forgive and understand the true reality and motivations that underlie all life-experiences. One who *acknowledges* reality simply views Universal Existence through the eyes of the God-self and knows that "All is as One". The soul incarnate who *acknowledges* reality allows all things to be and is then able to clearly perceive the elements of life. It is then that one can choose behaviors that conscionably impact upon The Greater Good of all things born of Creation.

The importance of understanding the difference in application between *acknowledging* and *judging* the elements of one's reality lies in the choice one makes to express his/her Reality of Truth through heart-centered behavior. What this means is that when a soul incarnate being chooses to engage the path toward enlightenment, he/she also chooses to embrace the revelation that both reactionary behavior and viewing life as a series of events charged by polarized energy states are counterproductive to the evolution of Light-mindedness. Therefore, as one awakens to embrace The Consciousness of One and evolves beyond the compelling drives of base and navel chakra orientation, one also learns to allow all things to simply be. One learns to flow with the experience of mortal life, without resistance or self-centered behaviors, for in so doing, one soon comes to find that The Oneness of Creation is an ever-expanding, Divine Expression of Universal Love. The time of readiness for each soul incarnate being to accept all aspects of life-conditions without *judgements* or reactionary behaviors most certainly will come to pass at the moment that is good and right in the evolutionary journey of each mortal being.

"... In order for mortal man to evolve beyond the drives of curiosity, mankind will need to surrender the compelling energies of the ego-self to The Greater Fulfillment of The Universal One."

Thirty-Seven

Q: Please comment about man's "curiosity" and the driving need to "figure out" the motivations, factors and designs of third dimension reality.

A: The curiosity that mortal man displays can indeed prove to be a two-sided coin. To be sure, it is good and right to uncover and to allow the elements of consciousness to be revealed in one's life-journey for the purpose of unfoldment in The Light of One. However, if one seeks to uncover the underlying factors of third dimension reality for the purpose of controlling aspects thereof, or for the purpose of establishing dominion over other soul incarnate beings, then the moment of curiosity clearly will have led to self-serving and counterproductive behaviors that will distort perceptions and influence subsequent behaviors.

When one engages impulses of curiosity, there are two questions that one can ask self to determine personal motivation: *"What is the purpose of my wanting to know?"* and, *"Is there a Greater Good to be served by my following this thought pattern?"* When answering these questions, one can quickly isolate personal motivation and see the designs of the ego-self at work, attempting to rationalize and/or to compel one to continue that which may ultimately prove to be an egocentric behavior pattern.

If one is engaging that which one believes to be curiosity for the sake of Spiritual Attunement and for the evolution of self, then, in truth, that which one has engaged is not the conscious mind and the ego-self at all. In truth, that which one has accessed are aspects of Intuitive Wisdom generated by the God-self. When one has accessed states of Intuitive Wisdom, though there may be desire to further understand the elements of one's reality, one will neither become impatient, nor will one become anxious and filled with a sense of urgency; rather, there will be acceptance of the natural order of unfoldment. The soul incarnate being will know that he/she is not in a race or competition with other soul incarnates and that the illusions of time, immediacy and urgency are devices and counterproductive elements of the conscious mind and the ego-self.

It is important to understand that in order for mortal man to evolve beyond the drives of curiosity, it will be necessary for mankind to surrender the compelling energies of the ego-self to The Greater Fulfillment of The Universal One. Then there can be a clear, undeniable, conscionable course of behavior implemented to transmute and/or to extinguish the conditioned behaviors and Karmic Debts that would inhibit the evolution of the God-self. It is then that each soul incarnate being can come to experience the Peace, Contentment and Fulfillment of "Inner Knowingness" that fills mortal consciousness with The Wisdom of One.

"... The most essential component ... is an open, Loving, heart-centered desire to release and transmute hostile, discordant energies with Compassion, Mercy and Understanding ..."

Thirty-Eight

Q: How does one respectfully decline etheric communications that one believes to be transmitted from a hostile source?

A: It is good and right for each soul incarnate being to choose with whom he/she wishes to commune, without fear, coercion or any undue pressure exerted upon one to accept any particularly doctrine or group consciousness. However, it is also good and right for mortal man to acknowledge the true realities of all things, without hostility, resentment, anger or other reactionary behavior. You see, it is also important for mortal man to acknowledge the reality of that which he/she perceives to be discordant with energies of Love, Compassion and Mercy and especially so as mankind moves closer to the moment of Harvest. With energies of Love, each soul incarnate can effectively dispatch energies of discordance without being disturbed, influenced or becoming a part of a dissonant, counterproductive scenario. Each soul incarnate being then comes to understand that the only efficient manner by which to transmute or release discordance is by embracing that which causes fear or revulsion with heart-centered, altruistic vibrations of Love.

When one suspects that he/she is communing with energies from hostile Etheric or Earthly sources, it is good and right to simply acknowledge the nature of the energy presence, thank it for its moment of communication, then ask it (not command it) to *"leave and return unto the place from whence it has come, to find its own moment of Peace."* Then bless the energy presence in The Name of Yahweh, by The Spirit of The Christ and bid it Peace by saying, *"Shalom."* We have found this procedure to be most effective in dispatching hostile energy states in a manner that is both respectful and in keeping with the principles of Universal Law. When this procedure is used in association with Cleansing Incenses or specially prepared Cleansing Bath Oils and/or Consecrated Water, even the most insidious, determined vibrations of hostility are gently released from mortal consciousness. It is to understand, however, that the most essential component of this procedure is an open, Loving, heart-centered desire to release and transmute hostile, discordant energies with Compassion, Mercy and Understanding, for to act with any other aim or motivation is to actively become a part of the very discordance that one has attempted to transmute.

"Hostile energy factions attempt to seduce ... (man) with illusions of power, wealth, control and pleasure by directing mortal consciousness toward behaviors that promise 'abundance' and 'prosperity' through 'manifestation'..."

Thirty-Nine

Q: Is it ever "good and right" to accept etheric communications that one believes to be self-serving and in opposition to The Council of Twelve?

A: It is a matter of conscience, of individual choice, as to the source from which one accepts information, for if one is in touch with his/her Intuitive self, then one most certainly knows that which is good and right in each and every aspect or situation of life. Further, it is not for any incarnate being to arbitrarily determine that which is or is not good and right or "proper" for any other soul incarnate being; rather, it is to point out that to engage and to accept information from hostile vibrations for any reason, no matter how accurate, useful or innocent such transmitted information might seem to be, is to engage energies that are designed to ultimately develop self-serving behavior patterns.

It has been our observation that when well-meaning soul incarnate beings accept information from sources that have not been identified as benevolent, the soul incarnates rationalize and delude self into believing that, "if the information is accurate and useful, then the source of the information must be benevolent in intent". In effect, the soul incarnate will have assumed that the source of the information must be a conscionable vibration of intelligence designed to assist in mankind's Spiritual Evolution and that the choice to accept such information is good and right. To be sure, this is not the case. When a soul incarnate being accepts information from hostile sources, no matter how accurate the information or how cleverly the information source is masked to appear as benevolent, one has entreated Etheric or Earthbound Vibrations that are designed to color judgements and sully perceptions of one's true reality.

You see, if the source from which one receives information is self-serving, then it most certainly opposes the application of Universal Law as practiced by The Council of Twelve. What this means is that if the source of Etheric and/or Earthly communications does not recognize the body of Universal Law as valid, then the source of such information will have as its directive to develop and maintain the state of ego-consciousness or egocentricity in mankind that will impede man's upward spiral toward the assimilation of The Wisdom of One.

Hostile energy factions attempt to seduce the consciousness of mortal man with illusions of power, wealth, control and pleasure by directing mortal consciousness toward behaviors that promise "abundance" and "prosperity" through "manifestation" and freedom from third dimension worries through the "mastery" of life-conditions. The words, abundance, prosperity, manifestation and mastery, have taken on new connotations of dominance, hedonism, manipulation and self-centeredness that were not the original applications of these words as used in true Spiritual Traditions. Through the intervention of hostile factions, these words now define behaviors linked to egocentricity and the development of the ego-self.

As has been stated elsewhere in this text, The Council of Twelve exists to guide, nurture and to assist mortal consciousness in the evolution of self in a manner that is non-invasive, born of Love, Compassion, Patience and Understanding, a manner that ensures that the process of Spiritual Unfoldment develops at a rate that is good and right for each soul incarnate being. In contrast, energies from hostile Etheric and/or Earthly sources that oppose the precepts of Universal Law seek to direct mankind toward behaviors that aggrandize the ego-self and create Karmic Debt, acting to delay the unfoldment of the God-self. It is merely to understand the foregoing elements of Truth when confronted by energy states offering information that could lead one into the behavior mode of self-service. It is merely to understand that each soul incarnate being makes choices in his or her journey that will either veil, or facilitate the true realization of The Universal One.

*"It is . . . to simply
engage the journey
of life with the
confidence and faith
that all one needs
to have or know
to effectively negotiate
third dimension
existence will be
accessible at a time
that is good and right."*

Forty

Q: Akhenaton, what must one do or how must one apply Spiritual Conscience in order to learn about one's true or ultimate purpose in life?

A: Each mortal being will learn of his/her true life-purpose as a function of evolution of self, which allows one to clearly see the road ahead that leads to the revelation of the God-self and The Wisdom of One. Each mortal being will access elements of consciousness that will facilitate the moment of Karmic Resolution and the subsequent transformation of the ego-self that in turn makes it possible for mankind's Light-minded nature to be revealed. It is the release of self from the drives and desires associated with material acquisition and physical comfort that removes the blinders from man's eyes and allows him/her to clearly perceive the truth of reality. The release of self from compelling energies of the ego-self further allows mortal man to comprehend the nature of The God's Divine Order, thereby strengthening the understanding of mankind's place and value in terms of Universal Function.

Let us be clear in communication, for when most soul incarnates speak of life-purpose, they are asking questions such as, *"What job will I hold in the future?"* or *"In what capacity will I ultimately choose to serve my brethren and Creation?"* or *"I'm not satisfied with my job or with my life, because I feel I'm supposed to be doing something else with my life, something to help people. When will I know what I'm supposed to be doing with my life?"* Questions such as these are both justifiable and understandable, but it is not for this one to answer through prognostication; rather, it is for each soul incarnate being to embrace his/her journey through life with Patience, Compassion, Conviction, Mercy, Love and Understanding, for in so doing, such questions find their moment of resolution from answers that arise from one's own Intuitive Wisdom, from one's own God-illumined Consciousness. It is for each soul incarnate being to simply engage the journey of life with the confidence and faith that all one needs to have or know to effectively negotiate third dimension existence will be accessible at a time that is good and right. It is for each soul incarnate being to know that the ultimate purpose of all things born of Creation is to find that moment of Peace, Harmony and Love when all things born of Creation consciously exist within The God Spirit as One.

*"It is to allow self
to be at Peace by
accepting parents
and family members
as they are and not
projecting illusions
or making judgements
of how one would wish
family members to be."*

Forty-One

Q: *How does one cope with family members, especially parents, who constantly interfere, attempting to control, manipulate and influence the chosen course of one's adult life?*

A: During the course of most every mortal being's development in incarnate life, there comes the time when he/she chooses to leave the protective nest of the nuclear family, spreading his/her wings to test the winds of life as a responsible, capable being in the eyes of society, but in many cases, the parents are unwilling to relinquish the "parenting role". You see, it is not uncommon for parents to define the greater part of self-worth and personal identity through the lifestyles, accomplishments and failures of their children. Such thought and behavior patterns are frequently the results of generation after generation of parent/child relationships in which strong control and direction of the child's behaviors by the parent "for the child's own good" was perpetuated. Each generation of parents (consciously or not) in some ways emulates the behaviors and parenting styles of their own parents or are influenced by their parent's attitudes and actions in child-rearing. In some cases, parents act in ways deemed to be "in the best interest of the child" long past the formative years, becoming intrusive, demanding and disrespecting their adult children's rights to privacy and Choice of Free Will.

It is to understand that parents will have chosen particular behavior patterns to assist in engaging the Karmic Past, just as, in like fashion, the child will have chosen his/her parents and subsequent life-situations by which to learn The Lessons of Existence. It is to understand that controlling, demanding, manipulative attitudes and behaviors seen in one's parents are in large part the results of conditioned thoughts and behaviors, (some of which may be the result of one's parent's own traumatic family experiences) influences of Karmic Debt and desires for the expression of the ego-self. It is to understand that even though one is and/or has been treated with disrespect, abuse and with energies that thwarted the evolution of self, the soul incarnate of true Spiritual Conscience will choose to greet such energies of discordance with Love, Compassion, Mercy and most of all with Forgiveness.

It is for each soul incarnate being to understand that to cope with disturbing, inhibiting family behaviors requires conscionable, benevolent avenues of resolution. As one learns how to release memories of repression and dominance, notions of self-importance, self-doubt and self-pity, one can embrace those who would attempt to control, manipulate or usurp one's Choice of Free Will in arms of Love, Compassion and Mercy. It is to understand that to forgive self for having chosen discordant scenarios by which to learn The Lessons of Existence is the first step toward forgiving parents and other family members for invasive, dissonant behaviors that will have colored one's judgements and will have instilled and/or reinforced counterproductive behavior traits in one's consciousness. It is to allow self to be at Peace by accepting parents and family members as they are and not projecting illusions or making judgements of how one would wish family members to be. It is to accept all realities as they are presented or revealed to one, for in so doing, mortal man learns how to accept all aspects of self.

"...Mankind continuously and inadvertently engages in behaviors that sustain reactionary patterns, thereby perpetuating man's systematic maintenance of the illusion of duality."

Forty-Two

Q: In other texts, you have discussed the principle that you term "Duality of Truth". How does this principle relate to the Hindu concept of "Maya"?

A: What we have described as Duality of Truth* is indeed similar in principle to the Hindu concept of Maya. We have presented Duality of Truth as the principle of opposites within third dimension that operate to maintain a balance of energy states within the system of Creation. It is the seeker of Spiritual Conscience who inevitably learns to accept the principle of opposites and who comprehends the efficacy of releasing self from the need to react to polarizing energies connected with mortal existence. It is then through the evolution of self that the earnest seeker ultimately becomes the sage, a conscious soul born of Wisdom and Truth who is One with all things born of Creation.

In Hindu Tradition, Maya is described as the "cosmic illusion of duality" that mortal consciousness recognizes as the opposing energies of life that effect balance

For additional information regarding the principle of "Duality of Truth", see the text, Discussions of Spiritual Attunement & Soul Evolution, Volume I, pages 7, 30-32.

within third dimension. Accordingly, it is mankind's predilection for judging the relative value or inherent goodness of these opposing energies that keeps mortal consciousness imprisoned by the emotional ebb and flow generated by the pursuit of goodness and the avoidance of that which is deemed to be discordant, unsuitable or counterproductive to personal growth or detrimental to conditions of well-being.

In mankind's attempt to surmount discordant energies, man has unwittingly become a part of the very energy systems that he/she would wish to extinguish. By engaging in reactionary behaviors that initiate aggression, resentment and hostility toward the energy state or behavior viewed as adversarial or counterproductive, mankind becomes increasingly more entangled in the web of Maya that stimulates and perpetuates judgemental and egocentric behaviors. You see, when behaviors, personality traits or energy states are judged and identified as inappropriate, harmful or discordant, mortal consciousness immediately begins to shield self or engages in activities designed to protect self from the perceived threat of discordance. The thought of defending self against the invasion of hostile, discordant energy systems perpetuates the illusion of duality, for as a direct result of thoughts and acts of defense, one generates fears, uncertainties and judgements of personal self-worth. One is then compelled to fight, deny or to seek escape from aspects of one's true reality, which requires acknowledgement and forgiveness in order for the soul incarnate to continue upon the path toward enlightenment. Therefore, mankind continuously and inadvertently engages in behaviors that sustain reactionary patterns, thereby perpetuating man's systematic maintenance of the illusion of duality.

When mortal consciousness evolves to the point where man is no longer willing to submit to and sustain counterproductive, conditioned patterns, then mankind will accept the proposition that The Light and the darkness exist as One. What this statement means is that as mankind learns and chooses to release self from the influence of reactionary behaviors designed to maintain, enhance or to impact upon states of the ego-self, mortal consciousness will approach the time of readiness to accept the reality that the continuum of emotions, behaviors and energy states encountered in mortal existence are designed to illuminate mortal consciousness with an understanding of Divine Purpose that transcends the single-minded elements of self-absorbed interest. When this time of readiness eventuates, mortal consciousness will no longer look upon discordance as an obstacle to Spiritual Unfoldment; rather, mortal man will embrace energy states of discordance with Patience, Compassion, Wisdom, Mercy, Serenity and Selfless Love and will graciously accept counterproductive vibrations as opportunities to strengthen Conviction and Purpose in The Light of One. It is then that mankind will execute the inherent responsibility charged to mortal consciousness - which is to transcend the cosmic illusion of Maya and to bond with The Living, Loving God Spirit pulsing in The Oneness of Creation.

"In our practice of Spiritualism, telepathy or Divine Thought is employed on a daily basis to invoke Benevolent Spirit Energies, to communicate with plants and animals and to transmit prayers ..."

Forty-Three

Q: *How do you define "Telepathy" and how it is used in the practice of Healing Facilitation and Spiritualism?*

A: Telepathy* is defined as the transference of thought vibrations or the conscious ability to communicate between two or more minds utilizing techniques other than conventional, mortal sensory modes. Techniques of telepathy have many applications in both the practice of Healing Facilitation and in the general practice of Spiritualism. Many times during the course of Facilitation/Counseling Sessions, a practitioner discovers through Intuitive and Divine Guidance that the client fears abandonment, being left alone to face the uncertain changes of the winds of life and holds the discordant memory of both childhood and past incarnate fear of abandonment in his/her heart chakra. It is detected by the practitioner that the energy matrix associated with the fear has caused tightness and a chronic painful throbbing sensation in the client's chest. (Previous medical examinations have revealed no

*For further discussions about "Telepathy", refer to the section entitled, "Telepathic Communications" in the text, Crystal Communion: LoveLight Meditations by Akhenaton.

organic problems that would cause these symptoms.)

Through visionary illumination, the facilitator/practitioner is shown actual sequences that occurred in the client's childhood, as well as past incarnate references to abandonment that quickly flash in the facilitator's consciousness. The facilitator does not speak directly about the visionary sequences that he/she has experienced; rather, the facilitator is moved to ask the client, *"What is it that frightens you? What is it that you fear?"* The client sits in silence, looking away from the facilitator and does not verbally respond to the question. The practitioner then asks, *"How does your chest feel?"* The client answers, *"There's tightness and pain, but it feels like something is pounding on my chest, a heavy weight or something . . . and the doctors can't find anything wrong with me."* The facilitator asks, *"Would you like to investigate the cause of the discomfort that you're experiencing?"* The client replies, *"Well, . . .yes."* It is then that the facilitator looks deeply into the client's eyes and communes with his/her soul consciousness.

Next, the practitioner asks the client to look directly into the practitioner's third eye, as the practitioner gazes into the client's third eye. Then the facilitator telepathically poses this question to the client's soul consciousness, *"Do you wish to uncover the core motivations for the feelings that are afflicting your body?"* Almost instantaneously, the facilitator will intuitively hear the answer, which in this case was, *"No, I'm afraid of what*

I'll find . . . No, not now, another time." The practitioner then transmits a telepathic blessing, a Divine Thought, that generates a warm, comforting, relaxing feeling throughout the client's body. To do any more than this would be to commit an unconscionable act of encroachment upon the client's Choice of Free Will. Nevertheless, the practitioner will have performed an act of service by generating a benevolent blanket of Loving Divine Light Vibrations to caress the client with Patience, Compassion, Wisdom and Mercy, which will ultimately stimulate a sense of understanding and support for the client in the execution of his/her future choices. This will also allow the client to recognize and accept the approaching time of readiness to release the burden of fear that he/she has been carrying. Additionally, the client will intuitively and sometimes consciously understand the nature of the blessing that was offered and it does happen on occasion that a client will acknowledge having heard the actual telepathic question asked by the facilitator.

It is also commonplace during Telephone Counseling/Facilitation Sessions to transmit Divine Light Energy to facilitate either or both general and specific conditions of well-being. By concentrating upon the client's name and communing with his/her soul consciousness, an experienced facilitator is able, By The Grace of The Universal One, to effect dynamic changes in the energy field and systems of consciousness that pervade the client's physical and auric bodies.

Through this process of telepathy that we term "Divine Thought", we are able to commune with, transmit messages or channel energies to clients without having to be in physical proximity to the soul incarnate to whom vibrations are directed. It is our regular practice to commune with clients in different parts of the country and through Divine Thought, we are able to offer Facilitation Services as the need arises.

Sometimes called Absentee Healing Facilitation, an evolved Spiritualist can generate Loving Energy and telepathically transmit these focused vibrations to assist other soul incarnate beings in negotiating the evolutionary journeys of the soul. In our practice of Spiritualism, telepathy or Divine Thought is employed on a daily basis to invoke Benevolent Spirit Energies, to communicate with plants and animals and to transmit prayers for Love, Peace and Fulfillment in The Light of One to our brethren, The Earth Mother and to all things born of Creation. Through focused, LoveLight Energies generated through an open, evolved heart chakra, an experienced Spiritualist can transmit or project these "higher octave" energies through conscious thought to any part of the globe or to any part of the Universe at any time. Such advanced abilities place significant responsibility upon the practicing Spiritualist to maintain firm grounding in The Wisdom of One. To be sure, when a Spiritualist reaches the stage of evolution at which telepathy is used regularly and is practiced with conscience, then the Spiritualist will have accepted The Sacred Covenant of LoveLight Transmission and will also have become an Initiate in The Light of The Universal One.

" … To engage in acts of facilitation requires that the practitioner achieves an active state of communion with The Universal Source of Divine Light Vibrations …"

Forty-Four

Q: Please define the Eastern concept of "Prana" and explain how this principle applies to the practice of Healing Facilitation.

A: In Hindu Philosophy, Prana is defined as the energy system that is the "Life-force" which pervades the Universe and is responsible for Creation. It is this Life-force Energy that we call Divine Light Vibration which can be channeled and infused into the physical and auric bodies of mortal man to transmute dysfunctional conditions during sessions of Healing Facilitation. To be sure, each soul incarnate being has an innate supply of Prana existing within his/her energy matrix, for by definition, this must be so. However, to engage in acts of facilitation requires that the practitioner achieves an active state of communion with The Universal Source of Divine Light Vibrations, or the reservoir of Prana that exists outside of the practitioner's personal supply of Life Energy. You see, for a practitioner to rely solely upon his/her personal supply of Prana for tasks of facilitation would ultimately lead to a severe depletion of the practitioner's vital Life Energy. Indeed, we are familiar with many cases in which practitioners of Bodywork and Energywork were forced to discontinue practices of facilitation due to the physical debilitation caused by loss of vital Life Energy that occurred as the result of the demands placed upon physical energy systems by acts of facilitation.

It is the ability of the practitioner of Healing Facilitation to bond with The Etheric, Life Energy Source that allows the act of facilitation to be successfully performed. As we have written elsewhere, mortal man "heals" nothing; rather, an evolved soul initiate chooses to allow his/her body to be used as an instrument for the transmission of Divine Light Vibrations, thereby acting as a humble participant, a conscionable element in The Divine Process of Healing. It is the direct result of the facilitator's understanding the nature and movement of this Life Energy or Prana that affects the level of success at which facilitations are performed.

As the practitioner/facilitator develops a broader, more detailed understanding about the dynamic nature of Prana through Meditation, visualization techniques and through the hands-on participation in acts of facilitation, one finds that his/her personal energy matrix becomes more refined, more attuned to the higher vibratory rates through which Prana is accessed. What this means is that the practitioner learns to raise his/her resonance rate to more closely approximate the resonance rate of The God Spirit. Physical changes in the body experienced by the practitioner due to the temporary elevation of resonance levels include:

increased body temperature, elevated blood pressure, pulsing waves of electrical energy enveloping the chakra cord and radiating through the body, dramatic convergence of the etheric and physical bodies, intensified perception modes, heightened conscious and intuitive channeling abilities and direct communion with The Living God Spirit.

As the practitioner becomes progressively more attuned to the higher vibratory rates, he/she experiences less and less stress or adverse impact upon the physical body as a result of raising resonance rates, for subtle metabolic and physiological changes will have occurred in the practitioner's energy matrix and bodily systems to accommodate the higher resonance pattern. Additionally, at this point of physical and Spiritual Evolution, the practitioner/facilitator can maintain this higher resonance rate for indefinite periods of time. It is at this level of consciousness that the Healing Facilitator not only understands the conscionable applications of Prana, but he/she will also have crossed the galactic threshold that leads to limitless Universal Knowledge. It is at this level of consciousness that the Healing Facilitator will have chosen to release the final remnants of the ego-self and will have become as One with all things born of Creation.

*"It is the choice
of each mortal being
to experience the depth
of various emotions
that will best facilitate
the learning of vital
Lessons of Existence
that are specifically
applicable to . . . the
evolution of self."*

Forty-Five

Q: *Akhenaton, you have discussed the nature of fear and mankind's need to experience all emotions enroute to Spiritual Unfoldment, but how does one overcome intense moods of sadness and depression? How does one cope with the desire to simply escape from one's life-condition? How does one find the fortitude and the will to continue life when shrouded by paralyzing sensations of anxiety, confusion and frustration?*

A: During the course of each soul incarnate being's journey toward the assimilation of The Wisdom of One, there will be moments of sadness and bouts with depression of varying degrees of intensity to negotiate. This is the normal course of events for the evolutionary journey that mankind has accepted. However, it is the choice of each mortal being to experience the depth of various emotions that will best facilitate the learning of vital Lessons of Existence that are specifically applicable to his/her incarnate experience and the evolution of self. Further, it is the function of Karma and the innate desire for Karmic Resolution within the consciousness of man that directs the emotional scenarios that each soul incarnate being must engage, comprehend and find viable applications for in his/her reality,

217

thereby finally releasing self from the need to engage similar situations of discordance by which to learn The Lessons of Existence. This is not to say that many soul incarnates do not experience debilitating feelings of sadness, frustration, confusion, anxiety and depression; rather, each mortal being allows various life-conditions to dictate emotional involvements in order to effect soul-level comprehension of the emotions involved, for the conscionable application of Divine Truth connected therewith to unfold and, while in the midst of adverse conditions, for the acknowledgement of one's personal connection to The Infinite Body of God to surface.

Emotional energies and the impact that these intensely compelling vibrations have upon mortal consciousness can be seen in the behaviors of many soul incarnate beings who feel as if they are being persecuted by society, are unable to reconcile that their personal realities are conditions of their own making and whose behaviors display an unwillingness to evolve beyond the moment of despair. You see, when mankind courts the whims of the ego-self, it is inevitable that in time the pit of self-indulgence will follow. Subsequently, during times of adversity and emotional stress man becomes prone to draping and shielding self with the soiled blanket of self-pity to avoid the responsibility of or to escape from the direct confrontation of emotionally charged issues. It is then that all one can see and experience is the immediate, choking, paralyzing reality of depression, anguish and despair. All perceptions and observations become compromised by the distorted drives of self-interest and one's sense of Godliness becomes diminished, spiraling ever downward, becoming obscured by the hollow illusions of need for personal advancement and personal worth. In effect, when the unbridled desires of the ego-self are allowed to direct behavior and consciousness, then it is inevitable that one will be led to engage Spiritual, mental and emotional energies that can severely damage and in some cases destroy one's hopes and desires for continued life during any given incarnation.

To extricate self from such moments of tribulation and pain requires that mortal man look beyond the immediate moment of personal comfort and desire. To release self from the pit of despair is to allow self to see and feel The Light of One glowing and pulsing in the depths of one's own being. To continue life when shrouded by anxiety, confusion and frustration is to surrender the single-minded, self-serving vision of mortal consciousness to The Galactic Vision of The Universal One. To do these things is to release self from the drives of competition, the acquisition of material wealth and the quest for physical gratification. To do these things is to allow the gradual, systematic extinction of the ego-self to eventuate and in so doing, mortal consciousness evolves to enjoy the God-illumined state of being, which acknowledges the blossom of Love arising from the ashes of despair.

*"In each and every
state of incarnation,
mortal man is
responsible for
everything that
he/she thinks,
feels and does."*

Forty-Six

Q: *Please explain the purpose of "Addictive and Abusive Behaviors" in the evolution of mortal consciousness.*

A: In each and every state of incarnation, mortal man is responsible for everything that he/she thinks, feels and does. This statement does not preclude the fact that during many states of incarnation, mortal man can be busily engaged in constructing emotional obstacles for him/herself that in some cases may appear to seriously impair or to completely arrest emotional development. Further, the motivation for such acts or choices that lead to continued situations of emotional discord may not be readily accessible by the conscious mind. This lack of understanding and control of one's feelings, behaviors and life-condition tends to lead one to question every aspect of one's reality and sense of self-worth. Such troubling feelings of uncertainty can easily compel one to seek validation for one's thoughts, feelings and actions from sources outside of self, which places one in an extremely vulnerable position. Frequently, because one has chosen to define reality of self based upon that which the external world arbitrarily confirms to be one's reality, mortal man encounters and displays behaviors that can be defined as either or both addictive (dependent or co-dependent) or abusive in nature.

Patterns of Karma play pivotal roles in influencing mortal man's choices of activities and behaviors and the subsequent feelings that arise concerning self-worth. Through investigation of past life behaviors, it is readily revealed that patterns of addiction, dependency and/or abuse had been established through prior incarnate behaviors and unbeknown to the conscious mind of the soul incarnate, he/she will be actively engaged in the process of Karmic Resolution in his/her present incarnation so as to free self from a particular lingering system of discordance. To be sure, for such a release to be effective and complete, the soul incarnate will have need to experience the depths of emotion and anguish associated with behaviors of abuse, dependency or addiction.

As with any discordant scenario, the purpose of these abusive and/or dependent behaviors is to assist mortal consciousness in assimilating specific Lessons of Existence. Even though the assimilation process can prove to be both physically and emotionally painful, it will have been the soul-level choice of each incarnate being who finds him/herself engaging scenarios of abuse and addiction to resolve the Karmic Debt associated with such painful behaviors. It is, as always, for each mortal being to accept his/her life-condition at face value, to allow self to comprehend the motivating factors for all aspects of one's conscious being through Meditation and Love in The Light of One and to allow self to release those aspects of consciousness that prove to be counterproductive. Through this process mortal man to learns to extinguish further need to engage additional moments of abuse and/or debilitating dependency in this or future incarnations.

"...There is nothing to fear - rather, there is everything to embrace; there is nothing to command - rather, there is everything to allow; there is nothing to judge - rather, there is everything to accept."

Forty-Seven

Q: *How do you define "Exorcism", Akhenaton, and what place does this procedure have in your practice of Spiritualism?*

A: Exorcism is the forcible ejection of that which is identified as an "unclean", angry or discordant disembodied spirit presence from the energy matrix of mortal man. The spirit presence that is exorcised will have invaded and attached itself to mortal consciousness with the intention of perpetrating hostile acts against Creation. These acts or behaviors are designed by discordant spirits to denigrate, draw life from or to destroy the sense of purpose and the beauty of the collective soul of Creation.

Rituals of exorcism have long been known to organized Religion as well as practiced in Tribal and Spiritual Traditions throughout the world. What is interesting to note is that in virtually all Traditions, the practice of exorcism unilaterally presupposes that man has the right to "command" spirit presence to act in ways that man would deem appropriate. Even though exorcism is performed to transmute a disembodied entities' willful invasion and hostile disregard for mortal man's Choice of Free Will, to engage in acts that aggressively attempt to command any spirit presence is contrary to our philosophy and practice of Spiritualism.

When we encounter energies that are hostile to the principles of Universal Law or are simply angry and intent upon making mischief, coloring mortal judgements or inflicting pain upon the body of Creation, instead of reacting to these vibrations with feelings and acts of aggression, we embrace them with the transformational benevolence of Love. We embrace even the most hideous, insidious vibrations of discordance with Love, Compassion, Patience and Mercy to assist in the release of these counterproductive energies or angry disembodied spirits from the consciousness of man.

In our view, it is neither our right, nor our responsibility to command anyone or anything; rather, that we selflessly bond with all things, which allows the physical body to be used as a Divine Tool for the transformation and transmutation of discordant energy. It is through the resonance of Love that we facilitate an evolutionary moment by offering both the hostile presence and its mortal host the vehicle by which to change the very nature of their energy matrices. To be sure, our participation is an act of service designed to respect the Choice of Free Will of both the discordant spirit presence and mortal man.

It is simply to understand that as children of Creation, mortal man has the responsibility of engaging life with

Conviction, Truth and Love. Further, it matters not if man discovers elements of Creation that appear to be hostile, self-serving or intent upon destroying the very fabric of life. It is to allow self to realize that all things born of Creation are One in The Eyes of The Universe. Therefore, there is nothing to fear - rather, there is everything to embrace; there is nothing to command - rather, there is everything to allow; there is nothing to judge - rather, there is everything to accept. When the consciousness of man is ready to assimilate these principles, then the thought and need of exorcism will become extinct, as then mortal man will naturally facilitate the transformation and transmutation of energy states that require such assistance.

"It is through the chakras or energy centers of the body that the balance of Life Energy is established and maintained for the effective operation of the physical and auric systems of mortal being."

Forty-Eight

Q: Please discuss the nature and function of the "Chakra System" and explain how the Chakra System is engaged to affect Healing Facilitation.

A: The Chakra System* regulates the flow of Life Energy (electrical energy transmissions that are vibrations of Divine Light Energy) throughout the physical and auric bodies of mortal man. It is through the chakras or energy centers of the body that the balance of Life Energy is established and maintained for the effective operation of the physical and auric systems of mortal being. With seven primary chakras located along the spinal column, five primary chakras situated above the physical body and twelve meridian chakras that govern the flow of energy along and to the extremities, the Chakra System is also designed to operate in concert with the organ systems of the body to sustain optimum conditions of well-being.

Based upon Knowledge from ancient Spiritual Traditions known especially to Eastern Cultures, individual chakras within this energy system can be

*See *Crystal Communion: LoveLight Meditations* under "Chakra System Dynamics".

229

observed to present any one of seven possible orientations that change in accordance with various physical, emotional, mental or Spiritual factors. Chakras can be determined to exist as: *open, closed, partially open, partially closed, blocked, shielded or sealed,* which dictates the manner in which the chakra bodies are to be approached to affect acts of Healing Facilitation. An *open chakra* indicates an area of general health and vitality or conditions of emotional development and stability. There is a warm, comforting energy presence of assurance that emanates from such a chakra. (Skilled practitioners of Healing Facilitation can detect chakra states by gazing upon the physical and auric bodies as well as scanning the chakra cord.) A *closed chakra* indicates an unwillingness to engage a specific area of consciousness that ultimately will have an adverse effect upon the corresponding area or organ system of the body. A *closed chakra* generates no significant volume or presence of energy sensations at all. Only the faintest possible energy presence or movement can be detected within a *closed chakra.* It is literally a lifeless area of one's being, an area of consciousness from which one may have detached in an attempt to avoid painful, problematic emotional memories and energy. A *partially open chakra* is one that results from a soul incarnate's moving through a time of emotional recognition, upheaval or engagement, yet there is a willingness to accept and to resolve the nature of the energy state in question, thereby transmuting problematic thoughts and behaviors which facilitates evolution.

A *partially open chakra* generates a diligent energy presence of warmth and hope. A *partially closed chakra* is the result of a soul incarnate being's finding self in the midst of emotional scenarios that the soul incarnate sees as overwhelming or as impossible to successfully negotiate or resolve. In an attempt to invalidate or to deny emotional impact, the soul incarnate begins to shut down or close off the chakra energy associated with the particular emotion. A *partially closed chakra* generates an energy presence of trepidation, uncertainty and dwindling hope. A blockage of energy can occur within or between chakras that is evidenced by an interruption of the flow of energy sensation within or between chakras or by a pulling or dragging sensation detected at any point along the chakra cord. (A *blocked chakra* can easily be confused with a *partially closed chakra*.) *Shielding of chakras* occurs as a reaction to any perceived, potential emotional energy that could inflict injury upon the energy matrix of man through the experience of life-situations. However, the *shielding* process actually implants within the Chakra System the very emotional energy that one would attempt to avoid, which leads to greater emotional discord than that generated by the original emotional state. Due to the fact that *shielding* is motivated by fear and by illusions maintained by the ego-self, the soul incarnate will unconsciously attempt to protect self from the perceived potential of emotional injury by generating cellophane-like membranes that cover the chakra or chakras associated with the perceived threat of emo-

231

tional injury. The highest state of chakra evolution is evidenced by *Chakra Sealing*.* *Chakra Seals* allow chakra energies to resonate at the highest possible rate during any one incarnation and act to facilitate clarity of perception and evolved integration of Etheric Truth with third dimension consciousness.

To accurately assess chakra conditions requires thorough understanding of subtle energy fields and the operation and function of emotional energies in mankind's journey of Spiritual Unfoldment. This is a task not to be taken as routine, for to engage in such practices requires Dedication, Conviction, Spiritual Evolution and Selflessness. (It should be noted that in the practice of Healing Facilitation, improper assessment of chakra states can lead to severe trauma to the energy matrix of mortal man. The indiscriminate, forcible invasion of chakra energy states can cause mental and emotional conditions of disassociation or detachment from one's physical consciousness and personal reality. Further, such potentially destructive actions can compromise the integrity of one's Life Energy and allow unspecified Earth and Etheric Energies to attach to one's auric and physical bodies. Such conditions of attachment can exert influence upon one's Choice of Free Will and decision-making process, which can present a difficult obstacle to surmount in

*See "Chakra Sealing & The Council of Twelve" in Crystal Communion: LoveLight Meditations.

232

the evolution of self.)

Skilled practitioners of Healing Facilitation analyze chakra states to help determine the operative dynamics of existing emotional conditions, the nature of physical dysfunctions and the level of Spiritual Evolution of those soul incarnate beings who seek assistance in uncovering core motivations for personal behaviors and life-conditions. When a skilled practitioner engages a client, his/her ability to utilize Intuitive/Spiritual Guidance in assessing the client's general state of well-being quickly becomes self-evident. An experienced practitioner will know the nature of one's Chakra System and the corresponding emotional and physical tendencies within moments of greeting the client.

Due to higher states of consciousness developed through Meditation practices and as the result of a willingness to encumber the pain and suffering of humanity for the purpose of assisting the collective evolution of man, an experienced facilitator can empathize with a soul incarnate's emotional matrix, identify and comprehend dysfunctions and make statements that gently guide the soul incarnate toward personal discovery of the nature of his/her dysfunctional states of consciousness. Additionally, the experienced facilitator can transmute the discordant energy of emotional trauma by accepting the transfer of energies of discordance into his/her own heart chakra, where the discordant energy is cleansed and blessed with The Love of The Light of One. The energy is then directed from the facilitator's body to the depths of Mother Earth or to the distant ether to find its moment of Peaceful resolution. It is this process of transmutation that transforms the nature of discordant energy and releases mortal consciousness from emotional trauma and the subsequent physical pain. Further, by utilizing the condition of the Chakra System as a diagnostic tool, the experienced facilitator can guide his/her clients into areas of consciousness that facilitate the true expression of the God-self state of being.

*"The Akasha
is the basic,
elemental material
from which all reality,
consciousness and
conditions of life
evolve."*

Forty-Nine

Q: *Please explain the concept of "Akasha" as it applies to Universal Creation, the flow of Life-force Energies and the development of The Consciousness of One.*

A: Akasha* is a Sanskrit term used in Hindu philosophy to define the etheric, elemental material from which all physical reality is formed. It is this subatomic, living material that forms the basic building blocks from which all Life-force Energies are realized. Through the "Creative Thought Process", The Universal God-Consciousness utilizes and directs the Akasha to fashion that which is the reality of all things within the bounds of Universal Existence.

The Akasha also retains the living memory of all aspects, functions and natures of consciousness ever existing throughout the Universe; that is, every event, thought and behavior that has ever existed since the beginning of time is etched upon the living memory of the Akasha. Known as the "Akashic Record", this body of Universal Knowledge and Evolutionary Archives can be accessed and reviewed by those soul incarnate

*See <u>Crystal Communion: LoveLight Meditations</u> under "Rhythmic Breathing".

237

beings who allow themselves to raise their resonance rates to attune to the Akashic Vibrations. By engaging the Akashic Record, mortal man can graphically see and feel the impact of past behaviors that formed the basis for present thought and behavior tendencies. Further, the Akashic Record holds information that can aid in the understanding of the evolution of consciousness, detailing the historical choices that mankind has made and how these choices have influenced the evolution of the collective soul of man.

The Akasha is the basic, elemental material from which all reality, consciousness and conditions of life evolve. It is the Akasha that is the living, God-Conscious energy of life that is the active essence of Universal Creation. By directing the flow and complexity of the Akasha, The Universal God-Head generates the Life-force Energies or Prana that fill the Universe with a "Life-essence" or potential for the generation and/or regeneration of Life/Light Consciousness. It is the result of reality precipitated by the Akasha from which all things of Creation are born. Therefore, all things born of Creation are bonded to each other by virtue of common birth, as all things contain the same Life/Light Consciousness that is the active essence of Akasha.

When we say, "All things are as One", we are alluding to the principle of The Consciousness of One or The Wisdom of One that acknowledges the kinship inherent to all Creation. It is through the structural and conscious essence of the Akasha that the reality of Oneness is acknowledged as Universal Truth. It is by virtue of the existence of the Akasha that Universal Creation has and continues to evolve. It is through the practical realization and acceptance of the existence and purpose of the Akasha that mankind can cement his/her understanding of Universal Life/Light Consciousness. It is through conscious bonding with the living, functional essence of the Akasha that mortal man can learn to identify and appreciate The Presence of The Spirit of God pulsing in the heart of Creation.

"...Psychometry... clairvoyance... Intuitive Wisdom and Divine Guidance each play contributing roles in the development or in the re-accessing of evolved perception skills."

Fifty

Q: *Akhenaton, how does it happen that some Spiritualists (such as you) can ascertain the basic personality traits and behavior tendencies of a person by simply hearing or seeing his/her name? Is this a type of "Clairvoyance" or "Psychometry"?*

A: In the present phase of mortal evolution, there are many soul incarnate beings who are learning to attune to a wide spectrum of vibrational frequencies, resonance rates and kinetic/potential energy transmission modes. These abilities or perceived "extra-sensory" talents are truly neither outside of the "normal" limits of the abilities that can be expected for an evolved soul incarnate being to display, nor are these skills or abilities "special gifts" bestowed upon a select few mortal beings by The Infinite One; rather, such skills of perception are directly attributable to past incarnate knowledge and practice of techniques that develop perceptual clarity, as well as individual readiness and willingness to open one's conscious being to access the memory (consciously or intuitively) of the use of various perception techniques. Indeed, this is the process undertaken to accomplish reading and comprehending the subtle energy states transmitted through each soul incarnate's birth or chosen name.

When we scan the energy presence that is transmitted through a soul incarnate's name, we perceive a blueprint of resonating energy patterns characteristically unique to that soul incarnate being's evolutionary state of consciousness. When we see his/her picture or hold an object that belongs to that soul incarnate, we perceive particular energy states that translate into specific behavior tendencies, attitudes and choices of Karmic Evolution. In effect, through the resonating energy states that define the memory matrix of the soul, we are allowed to commune with the soul essence of the soul incarnate being in question and access a visual reference of his/her state of consciousness, motivations in life, emotional condition and evolutionary stage.

Many times we are given past incarnate references associated with such a reading that assist us in focusing upon and relaying specific elements of importance to the unfoldment of a soul incarnate's emotional/mental/spiritual matrix. (It should be noted that information accessed through the use of these skills is held with the highest amount of respect and propriety and is never used in any way to manipulate or to compromise Choice of Free Will. Additionally, Choice of Free Will is not encroached upon at any time - either during the reading of resonating energy patterns, or during communication with the soul essence of an incarnate being.)

To further define these skills, we would say that psychometry, which is the ability to perceive information about an incarnate being or object by coming in contact with an object held by that incarnate being, clairvoyance, which is the ability to perceive information that is not readily discernable by the senses through conventional processes of detection, Intuitive Wisdom and Divine Guidance each play contributing roles in the development or in the re-accessing of evolved perception skills. When a soul incarnate being is willing to embrace the Universe in a selfless manner, doors of enlightened consciousness begin to open, one after the other, for those incarnate beings who choose to serve the needs of Creation, instead of focusing upon the single-minded drives of the ego-self. As mortal man chooses to evolve and release self from counterproductive, conditioned drives of the ego-self, a greater understanding of Universal Processes naturally unfolds. Therefore, the elements of psychometry, clairvoyance, Intuitive Wisdom and Divine Guidance are allowed to unite to facilitate heightened clarity of perception that further facilitates greater insights and additional opportunities to offer conscionable assistance in the evolution of the soul of man.

"... The use of profanity literally calls forth hostile energies or attracts discordant vibrations toward one like a magnet."

Fifty-One

Q: *What impact does the use of profanity have upon the course of one's evolving Spiritual Consciousness?*

A: The use of profanity generates an energy pattern that stimulates conditions conducive to the aggregation of hostile, discordant energies (be they thought or behavior patterns or spirit presence), which can precipitate subtle or dramatic influences that can prove to be counterproductive to the processes of enlightenment and the evolution of self. In effect, the use of profanity literally calls forth hostile energies or attracts discordant vibrations toward one like a magnet. This in turn nurtures the development of problematic behaviors that act to compromise the course of the expression of the God-self. Clearly, beckoning or drawing discordance toward one appears to be counterproductive, but depending upon one's need and stage of evolution, the discordance attracted by a soul incarnate being can ultimately prove beneficial in assisting one to break free from the Karmic patterns of dissonant behaviors.

It is to understand that the acts of cursing one's brethren or using profanity to express one's emotional feelings are by definition acts of aggression and hostility. It is a simple matter of deduction to realize that through acts of aggression and hostility, mortal man establishes patterns of behavior that tend to perpetuate further thoughts and acts of discordance. The time will come, however, when man deems it necessary to acknowledge the far-reaching implications of discordant behaviors that he/she may have looked upon as harmless, for the unseen vibrations connected with profanity can have an adverse effect upon the collective evolving consciousness of mankind. You see, it is not that the soul incarnate being who uses profanity to express him/herself is creating discordant patterns for him/herself alone, but that the use of profanity generates veils of disquieting, hostile energy around all who hear and feel the vibrations of expletives used increasingly in daily speech throughout many segments of society.

Those soul incarnate beings who are sensitive to subtle energy states can easily "tune in" and feel physical pain as a result of hearing profanity. This may seem a bit extreme, but in truth we do not exaggerate. Many gentle soul incarnate beings have been emotionally, spiritually and/or physically injured (not simply offended) by hearing profanity spoken in close proximity to them.

Though it is doubtful that there can be irreparable damage inflicted upon one's energy matrix by the vibrations generated through profanity, it is certain that one who proclaims self to be pursuing the Spiritual

Path toward enlightenment is only deluding self by allowing profanity to be a part of one's expression of self. Those soul incarnate beings who are earnest seekers of enlightenment quickly learn to transmute counterproductive, hostile behavior patterns for the sake of The Greater Good of all things born of Creation and in so doing, earnest seekers ultimately find Love, Peace and Fulfillment awaiting them in The Gracious Bosom of The Universal One.

"Only through heart-centered thoughts and behaviors can mortal man exist within The Conscience of One . . ."

Fifty-Two

Q: *Akhenaton, there are those soul incarnates who make statements and ask questions such as, "I've been 'on The Path' for more than ten years now, but there's just so much that I still don't understand. When will I find Peace and Happiness? When will I have clarity of perception and understand the nature and purpose of my journey?" How do you respond to such statements and questions?*

A: The road toward Understanding may lead one through the jagged cliffs of confusion, frustration and uncertainty before revealing the sweet-scented valley of Patience. It is for each soul incarnate being to pause long enough along the way to savor the moment of Patience and to learn how to embrace Patience as the eternal companion and teacher that it truly can be. It is for each mortal being to learn to transmute problematic energies of anxiety, desire and impulsiveness to find that Patience was quietly awaiting discovery. It is for each child of Creation to engage his/her journey with a sense of wonderment and graciousness, neither taking self seriously, nor engaging in self-importance, for it is through selfless perceptions of reality and by allowing self "to be" that mortal man experiences the revelation of Peace and Fulfillment.

Frequently, we see or are told about the overwhelming depths of frustration, confusion and uncertainty that plague many, many soul incarnates as they attempt to assimilate The Wisdom of One. Let us simply address this issue by stating that the conscious mind operating through the direction of the ego-self cannot comprehend, assimilate or vibrate in Harmony with The Wisdom of One. For one to think otherwise is by definition in contradiction to the very nature of the ego-self. Further, it is to accept the reality that "wanting" the perceived benefits of enlightened states of consciousness for personal development is a delusion perpetrated by the ego-self to achieve conditions of mastery and dominion over aspects of one's physical reality. Therefore, the delusion and distortion of reality committed by the ego-self is the insistence by the ego-self that it is good and right to seek Spiritual Truth for the reason promoted as personal evolution. However, in fact, the choice to seek Spiritual Truth will have been made for the singular purpose of attempting to elevate the status of the ego-self in terms of power and control, instead of pursuing The Spiritual Path for the sake of achieving union with The God Spirit alive in all things born of Creation.

Only through heart-centered thoughts and behaviors can mortal man exist within The Conscience of One, for it is only through an open, evolved heart chakra that Light-minded behaviors evolve. So you see, it matters not if one believes that he/she has been "on The Path" for 10 years or for 10,000 years, for the moment of awakening will not occur until one chooses to accept all aspects of self and to release the ego-self and the conditioned thoughts, behaviors and emotional reactions connected therewith. Only after this most important moment of acknowledgement and surrender occurs will one have taken his/her first, true step upon The Path of Enlightenment.

- ACKNOWLEDGMENTS -

In acknowledgement of The Council of Twelve,
The Spirits of Yahweh and The Christ,
and The Consciousness of The Infinite One,
for without the Illumination from These
this text could not have been undertaken.

Akhenaton

For the long hours of typesetting and proofreading;
For trusting even when understanding eluded you;
For accepting reality even when shrouded by
  illusions and fears;
For seeing the beacon of Truth shining in the distance
  and having the courage to walk with us into
  The Light of One -

Thank you, Gail, for all that you are,
For all that you shall eternally be.

Akhenaton

YMMI

For your steadfast devotion,
your selfless gifts of time,
Love and resources,
we thank you, Gentle One -
Be Thee Kept in The Light of One.
Shalom

LGF

For your generosity, Love and commitment
to sharing The Wisdom of One, we thank you -
Be Thee Kept in The Light of One.
Shalom

Through the generous contributions,
expressions of Love and gifts of time and labor
received from our patrons and associates,
the door at Portal Enterprises has remained open
to offer service to the needs of our brethren.

To you, our family, friends and supporters
- Kindred Spirits all -
we thank you -
Shalom,

Akhenaton

TESTIMONIALS

"... *There is much I would like to say,*
And in time, it will be said
But for now, let it be known
That to know him (Akhenaton) is to seek yourself
To seek him (Akhenaton) is to know yourself.
Although my association with Akhenaton has been limited in
this present incarnation, I know there is a kindness and gen-
tleness in Akhenaton that brings inner peace to those he
touches.

For me, he was a 'beacon of Light' when I needed assistance.
I will be forever grateful for knowing him."

H. Thompson
Baltimore, Maryland

"*Since I've seen Akhenaton, I can't explain how the tight-*
ness I used to feel in my chest has eased. It feels like my
heart has opened up like a flower . . . I promise I will never
forget him."

D. Michael
Los Angeles, California

"... *The purity and beauty of the Love Akhenaton so will-*
ingly emanates has been of great guidance to me as I travel
along my spiritual path . . . May God continue to bless
Akhenaton and his work in the honor and glory of 'The
One'."

Y. Dick
Cambridge, Massachusetts

". . . My unwillingness to accept my father's death, to 'let him go', was causing me physical pain and illness. The doctors didn't know what to do with me . . . Within an hour with Akhenaton - not days or months - I was freed of the pain and agony that had been 'choking' me for years . . . I am now more open to feel the needs of others rather than dwelling on myself.

I thank you, Akhenaton!"

P. Owens
Haymarket, Virginia

". . . Akhenaton is truly a blessing for he confirms Spiritual Truths that I know to be, and by him I am encouraged to share God's Truth with others."

B. Towell
Ashton, Idaho

"Akhenaton's Loving Touch Workshops have helped me move past the limiting beliefs of conditioned fear and have helped me to learn how to follow my own heart-centered vibrations of Truth. The experience of feeling and identifying chakra conditions have given me greater understanding that has opened new ways for me to share Love with others."

G. Lancaster
Clinton, Maryland

"Akhenaton is a truly gifted counselor and Healing Facilitator who shares his wisdom in a Loving, down-to-earth, and compassionate way . . ."

K. Franklin
Columbia, Maryland

"Akhenaton's joyful and deeply intuitive nature enables him to express his wisdom in ways that touch me with an understanding beyond the intellect alone. His gentle clarity encourages beautiful and exciting realizations in his students. Of all his many generous gifts, I most cherish his helping me to reconnect with The One."

P. Warren
Columbia, Maryland

"When I first met Akhenaton, I knew immediately that he was a man of total integrity and honesty. After just one session of Akhenaton's Healing Facilitation and balancing of my energies, there have been amazing and profound changes in my life.

Akhenaton is truly doing God's work, and I unreservedly recommend his services to anyone who is fortunate enough to contact him. Akhenaton has deeply touched my life and soul."

F. Logrando
South Fork, Pennsylvania

"Walking into Portal Enterprises was like walking into pure Love energy. As I turned to look at the beautiful stones that surrounded me, Akhenaton entered the room with a Loving energy surrounding him. Visiting Portal Enterprises will enlighten you as to how much Love there really is in this world. Akhenaton has a purity and a Love-Light radiating from him, and as you leave, you find that some of his Love leaves with you."

M. Brown
Catonsville, Maryland

"Akhenaton is an extraordinary human being who exemplifies the spiritual qualities which I strive to develop in myself. He has been a blessed resource, friend and teacher. His clarity helps me to find the clarity in myself. Likewise, his centeredness assists me in reaching my own center. In his presence, I feel Loved, accepted, valued, and most importantly, recognized for the beautiful spiritual being that I am (and which all of us are). Akhenaton is a spirit who truly gives freely and who provides his service to humanity with humility, devotion and deep, deep Love."

D. Martin
Glenelg, Maryland

". . . I always find a sense of peace at Portal Enterprises that I find nowhere else, and I get the answers and guidance that seem to be exactly what I need at the time that I need them.

. . . My earthly and spiritual respect for Akhenaton is beyond measure. I believe I was intuitively directed to him. Akhenaton has made a significant difference in my life, and I know he always will."

S. Smith
Columbia, Maryland

"Having participated in Akhenaton's LoveLight Meditation course was a 'highlight' in my life. The serenity with which Akhenaton conducted the course allowed everyone, experienced and inexperienced in meditation, to reach new levels of spirituality. Akhenaton gave me a gift that I will use and cherish for the rest of my life."

S. Keilholtz
Clarksville, Maryland

"Total freedom and ultimate joy have been mine since living my life in The Light of One. Akhenaton, in his gentle, Loving way, assists me in releasing all acknowledged discordance. To fly on the wings of Golden Eagle is to know all that we are - and always have been. Through Akhenaton I have learned that the Love we give is the Love we live."

C. Kellum
Columbia, Maryland

"During the time I have known Akhenaton, I have attended his LoveLight Meditation Classes, Sunday Spiritual Gatherings, read his books and benefited from personal counseling and Facilitated Healing. I have experienced his devotion to sharing with others and his dedication to his fellow beings. He has helped me to remember that we are One - with Spirit, with Mother Earth, and with each other."

M. T. Gray
Phoenix, Arizona

". . . I find that every session with Akhenaton is a new experience filled with teachings that inspire me more and more ."

R. Ndau
Silver Spring, Maryland

"In all my experience of teachers, both Spiritual and Secular, none have come close to the magnanimous giving of self and knowledge as Akhenaton. It is truly my privilege and a blessing to have been led to such a shining Light. Akhenaton, from the depths of my heart, I thank you!"

P. Chenier
Columbia, Maryland

261

"Akhenaton's knowledge and skill with Quartz Crystals affords him great abilities in Healing Facilitation, balancing and grounding of individuals . . . As a result of Akhenaton's facilitations, I've released blockages found in my throat and heart chakras, and now I feel a fullness of health and well-being . . . I am truly delighted as well as blessed to have been a participant in his Divine work."

L. Mondowney-Bey
Baltimore, Maryland

"I came to Akhenaton and Portal Enterprises searching for an answer, for a reason. What I found was inner peace, understanding and wisdom - all generated by Love. Now, I am filled with so much Love that I glow. I found what I was searching for."

S. Fields
Columbia, Maryland

". . . Akhenaton touched the soul of the Universe with me and shared his wisdom in such a Loving way ."

L. Earles
Columbia, Maryland

"The guidance I've received through continuing workshops with Akhenaton, private counseling and learning to develop sensitivity to my inner voice by practicing meditation has helped me to make better decisions for myself. My life is happier, more Loving and less anxious as I continue to learn to live through these practices."

K. Taylor
Columbia, Maryland

"Akhenaton is a gentle, caring soul, filled with Love and with a rich desire to reach out to the masses. His books have helped many on their quest for enlightenment. He has been and remains a true and trusted friend."

P .J. Miles
San Angelo, Texas

"Akhenaton has dedicated his heart and his life to assisting the evolution of each soul he meets."

A. Goldberg
Columbia, Maryland

To those beloved souls who took the time to express their feelings about our work, we humbly thank each of you for your Love, Kindness and Encouragement - Be Ye Kept In The Light of One.
Shalom

SPECIAL NOTES

The author and publisher welcome comments regarding the nature and content of this text. Akhenaton will personally answer letters received by the publisher. Please address comments to Akhenaton c/o:

THE PORTAL PRESS
P. O. Box 1449
Columbia, Maryland 21044

Additional copies of this text can be obtained from the publisher by sending $12.95 plus $2.35 postage and handling for each copy to the address above. *(Maryland residents please include 5% sales tax.)*

OTHER BOOKS BY AKHENATON

Creation's Promise: Journey Within The Light
(ISBN) 0-9621839-0-3
$8.95 plus $1.95 postage and handling *(per copy)*

Discussions of Spiritual Attunement & Soul Evolution, Vol. I
(ISBN) 0-9621839-1-1
$4.50 plus $1.50 postage and handling *(per copy)*

Crystal Communion: LoveLight Meditations
(ISBN) 0-9621839-4-6
$17.95 plus $3.45 postage and handling *(per copy)*

PORTAL ENTERPRISES
CRYSTAL GALLERY CATALOG

Portal Enterprises offers a unique selection of Quartz Crystals, Minerals and Spiritual Tools that have been cleansed, blessed and prepared by Akhenaton for use by those soul incarnates on The Path toward Enlightenment. Through Akhenaton, each Crystal, Mineral and Spiritual Tools is charged with Divine Light Vibrations to enhance and to elevate the resonance pattern of each item handled by Akhenaton and blessed in The Light of One. This additional preparation ensures that all items offered through the Portal Enterprises Crystal Gallery Catalog will resonate at optimum efficiency and intensity within the spectrum of Divine Light.

To receive a Portal Enterprises Crystal Gallery Catalog simply write to PORTAL ENTERPRISES, P. O. Box 1449, Columbia, Maryland 21044 or call us at (301) 317-5873.

A WORD ABOUT AKHENATON

An Illuminated Spiritualist, Teacher and a dedicated servant to the needs of Creation, Akhenaton is an Initiate of The Light of One who has come with the directive of sharing Love and The Wisdom of One with all mankind. Fully aware of his past incarnate history in Egypt, India, Tibet, Asia, North America, Atlantis and Lemuria, Akhenaton calls upon Intuitive Wisdom and conscious knowledge from many Spiritual Traditions to facilitate moments of Spiritual Awakening in those soul incarnate beings who seek his counsel. Akhenaton has dedicated his life to assisting in resolving the paradox that separates the mental, physical, emotional and spiritual aspects of mortal consciousness and in so doing, facilitate the experience of balance and harmony between the elements of self.

As an empathetic facilitator, Akhenaton willingly embraces and transmutes the pain and sadness, the confusion, frustration and anxiety, the fear, anger and resentment he uncovers that compromise the thoughts, feelings and behaviors of those he counsels. Akhenaton engages each day of life with Selflessness and through Illumination from and Communion with The Council of Twelve and The Yahweh Entity, Akhenaton performs acts of facilitation and participates in the experience of life with Wonderment, Love and Joy. With Gentleness, Wisdom, Compassion and Love, Akhenaton welcomes all things born of Creation with The Blessing of The Universal One filling his heart. With Patience, Mercy and Serenity, Akhenaton acknowledges and accepts the reality of that which is and allows all things to simply "be".

The LoveLight Invocation/Blessing

Given to Akhenaton by The Council of Twelve, The LoveLight Invocation/Blessing and segments thereof are employed in every facet of the work engaged and services rendered through Portal Enterprises. The Name, Yah, is used to invoke a particular, nurturing presence of The Yahweh Entity and the specific Archangelic Energies invoked facilitate access to the resonance of The Legion of Light.

Almighty Yah, Great Spirit of Light,
By The Spirit of Christ Jesus, in Thee do I trust.
Protect me, Father;
Guide me, Father;
Strengthen me, Father;
Cleanse me, Father;
Heal me, Father.
Fill me with The Light of Thy Presence, Father.
Surround me, Father, with
Archangel Michael in the East,
Archangel Gabriel in the West,
Archangel Raphael in the North,
Archangel Uriel in the South
and grant me communion, Father,
with Thy Legion of Light.
Almighty Yah, Great Spirit of Light,
By The Spirit of Christ Jesus, in Thee do I trust.
Amen.

271

The way of Selflessness is not the path
of the martyr;
Rather, the path of Selflessness is the choice
of the saint . . .

It is just to Know,
Just to Allow,
Just to Be.

In The Name of Yahweh,
By The Spirit of The Christ,
Be Ye Kept in The Light of One.

Shalom,

Akhenaton